BUT I PRAYED FOR THIS

BUT I PRAYED FOR THIS

WHAT TO DO WHEN LIVING IN GOD'S YES IS HARDER THAN YOU EXPECTED

MELISSA MILLER

NELSON BOOKS
An Imprint of Thomas Nelson

But I Prayed for This

Published by Nelson Books, an imprint of Thomas Nelson, 501 Nelson Place, Nashville, TN 37214, USA. Nelson Books and Thomas Nelson are registered trademarks of HarperCollins Christian Publishing, Inc.

Melissa Miller is represented by the literary agency of The Blythe Daniel Agency, Inc., PO Box 64197, Colorado Springs, CO 80962.

Thomas Nelson titles may be purchased in bulk for educational, business, fundraising, or sales promotional use. For information, please email SpecialMarkets@ThomasNelson.com.

HarperCollins Publishers, Macken House, 39/40 Mayor Street Upper, Dublin 1, D01 C9W8, Ireland (https://www.harpercollins.com)

Library of Congress Cataloging-in-Publication Data

Names: Miller, Melissa, Writer author
Title: But I prayed for this : what to do when living in God's yes is harder than you expected / Melissa Miller.
Description: Nashville, TN : Nelson Books, [2026] | Summary: "Melissa Miller explores how you can care for your soul, let go of guilt, and give yourself grace when your answered prayers bring changes you didn't expect and feelings you can't ignore"-- Provided by publisher.
Identifiers: LCCN 2026011720 (print) | LCCN 2026011721 (ebook) | ISBN 9781400254804 trade paperback | ISBN 9781400255672 ebook
Subjects: LCSH: Prayer--Christianity | Christian life
Classification: LCC BV220 .M55 2026 (print) | LCC BV220 (ebook)
LC record available at https://lccn.loc.gov/2026011720
LC ebook record available at https://lccn.loc.gov/2026011721

Art direction: Darren Samuel
Cover design: Lindy Kasler
Interior design: Kristina Juodenas

Printed in the United States of America

26 27 28 29 30 LBC 5 4 3 2 1

To my children, my five greatest gifts.
May you trust God when his answer is "no,"
wait on him when it's "not yet,"
and be sustained by his grace in every "yes."

CONTENTS

INTRODUCTION

So your prayer was answered, and your feelings aren't falling in line? Your dream was fulfilled, but the calling is much harder than you'd hoped? Welcome to something we all experience but rarely feel liberty to talk about. After all, we don't want to sound ungrateful—this is what we prayed for.

Well, friend, pull up a chair and have a seat, because there's no judgment here. In fact, let's make a deal: I'm going to assume you are grateful for your new blessings, if you assume the same about me. Like me, you've probably got a gratitude journal and seldom start a prayer without first thanking God. So let's start out with this baseline: We are grateful people. We are grateful to God, we aren't complainers, and we know we are living in the days that we once prayed for. That's all true. And do you know what's *also* true? Change is hard. Period.

Most people assume that change is hard only when it involves a loss, crisis, or tragedy. But some of the hardest changes are the good changes, because they can blindside us with their emotional weight. When the expectation of how we are supposed to feel and the reality of how we actually feel don't align, we wrap ourselves in guilt for feeling anything other than gratitude (and carrying a backpack full of guilt doesn't help our predicament).

Maybe the spouse you prayed for is here, but you discovered

that marriage is hard work. The baby you prayed for arrived, but you haven't slept since. The big dream you prayed for came to fruition, but now you're overworked and overwhelmed. *Isn't an answer to prayer supposed to feel better than this?*

As for me, I prayed for an exciting opportunity across the country, but when I made the move, I woke up every morning wondering, *What have I done?* I never expected to have such a hard time adjusting to my new surroundings. I prayed to adopt a child for over five years and, to my surprise, ended up adopting two—a double blessing that doubled my feelings of inadequacy. I thought I was fully prepared. I went to all the adoption conferences, trainings, certifications, and seminars. I expected to feel like I was made for this, but instead I felt like God had picked the wrong person. What happens when you get what you prayed for, but it feels different than you expected? What do you do when God said yes, but your heart feels like a mess?

To add to your tangled emotions, you might also be thinking, *Do I dare talk about this when God has bigger problems in the world to solve?*

I hold that tension with you, my friend. When your newsfeed is full of political unrest, war outbreak, and economic uncertainty, it can be hard to admit you're struggling with something that's good. Well, here's a different way to think about it: Perhaps the 24-7 access we have to all the world's turmoil in a six-by-three-inch device in our pockets is one more reason why our hearts feel heavy even while our hands hold a blessing. Our phones have taught us how to numb our emotions but not how to process them. We have become desensitized to things that should shock us, and we are emotionally short-circuiting because of it.

Yes, humanity needs help, but you are also one of those humans. The world needs healthy souls, and yours is included. God's grace isn't limited or portioned out only to those who need it most each day. Today, grace is available for you too—even if your problems seem small in comparison to your neighbor's.

It takes time to learn that it's not selfish to bring our honest emotions to God; it's sacred. After all, we feel the freedom to be the most honest with the people we feel closest to. Perhaps this season is an invitation from God to see him as one of those people—the softest place to land with the emotions you're most afraid to admit. Taking your feelings to God doesn't mean you're ignoring the world's pain, but rather that you're learning how to tend to your own heart so you have something real to offer a hurting world.

There is a better way to handle our human emotions than staying wrapped in guilt, attempting to bypass our feelings, or faking it until we make it. Through my whirlwind of change, I found myself springing so many emotional leaks, I became a walking sprinkler system. So I decided to stop pretending and face my confusing emotions head-on. I dove into therapy, research, and Scripture—and even humor—and learned how to show up in a story that felt different from what I imagined.

THE FOUR SEASONS OF BLESSING

As I began research for this book, I noticed similarities in those who started living in God's yes. I discovered that they all fell into different categories—or seasons—when they had received an answer to prayer. Scripture tells us, "There is a time for everything, and a season for every activity under the heavens . . . a time to weep and a time to laugh, a time to mourn and a time to dance."* Sometimes

* Ecclesiastes 3:1, 4

the first step to finding your way forward is naming the season you are in. I call these seasons of answered prayer the Four Seasons of Blessing. They include a Season of Blooming, a Season of Building, a Bittersweet Season, and a Season of Balancing.

1. **A Season of Blooming.** A Season of Blooming is when everything is in alignment: Your expectations meet your reality, your feelings are flourishing, and you are thriving in your answered prayers. You aren't experiencing mixed or mismatched emotions, you weren't thrown any curveballs, and you aren't grinding or exhausted. This is a sweet season of life that we all hope for; it's what we expect an answer to prayer to be like. You probably didn't pick up this book if you are blooming perfectly.

   In 1 Chronicles 4:10 we read a little story about a man named Jabez who prayed and seemed to receive the answer to his prayer without a hitch. "Jabez cried out to the God of Israel, 'Oh, that you would bless me and enlarge my territory! Let your hand be with me, and keep me from harm so that I will be free from pain.' And God granted his request." Jabez experienced the happily-ever-after we anticipate. We all want the key to unlocking this mess-free, end-of-story kind of blessing in our lives, but assuming that God's blessings will always result in a Season of Blooming is what unfortunately tangles our emotions. When Jabez's experience doesn't match ours, we might find ourselves in one of the other seasons . . .
2. **A Season of Building.** A Season of Building is when your answer to prayer comes with a lot of hard work. You're supposed to be living the dream, but most days you're living drained.

In the book of Nehemiah in the Bible, God answered Nehemiah's prayer to rebuild the walls of Jerusalem and granted him favor with the king. Rebuilding the wall was a meaningful assignment for Nehemiah; God answered a deep cry of his heart. But the rebuilding process didn't come without opposition, and the workers grew weary because there was so much rubble to move. This story from Scripture is how it sometimes feels walking out God's plan. We are grateful, but we are also grinding.

Those who are in a Season of Building need to recognize the weight of their work. They need to find the strength to build in the natural what they prayed for in the spiritual.

3. **A Bittersweet Season.** You might be in a Bittersweet Season if your answered prayer comes wrapped in both beauty and pain. It's when you experience mixed emotions and want to find a way to enjoy your new blessing while simultaneously grieving a loss or walking through a trial.

   In 1 Kings 18 Elijah prayed for God to show his power at Mount Carmel, and fire came down from heaven. It was a victorious moment, and he probably thought it would result in a neat and tidy resolution to his prayer like Jabez's "God granted his request." Period. But instead Elijah was thrown a curveball. He was sent a death threat that made him so fearful and discouraged that his next move was not celebrating; it was hiding. If you've ever wondered, *Why now, God?* you are not alone.

   Sometimes life brings something bitter while you're holding something sweet, and it doesn't check your calendar first.

4. **A Season of Balancing.** You might be in a Season of Balancing if you find yourself thinking, *Everything's fine, but I'm*

not. You've received your answer to prayer, and even though nothing is wrong on the outside, everything feels off on the inside. In the Old Testament Moses should have felt honored and excited to be chosen to lead Israel to the promised land, but instead he felt unqualified and wanted God to pick someone else. And the Israelites? They'd been set free from slavery. But instead of rejoicing, they grumbled and missed their old life. Aren't you supposed to feel confident when God chooses you? And why would anyone miss their old life when they got the good change they prayed for? It turns out, humans have had a hard time adapting to change as far back as the ancient world, and you're not the only one who "should" feel different.

You are in a Season of Balancing if you are trying to balance your mismatched emotions and are seeking clarity, alignment, and a way forward without the guilt.

—

As with most things in life, your season might not fit perfectly into one lane. You might be experiencing some overlap; maybe your Season of Building has also come with some balancing, or your Bittersweet Season also requires a lot of building. The goal of these labels isn't to create perfect descriptions but to open a dialogue that helps you identify your experience and name your emotions.

I've learned that just because something is blessed doesn't mean it comes without a mess. Both can be true. This book is your invitation to be honest about where you are and to find your way forward. No matter what season you find yourself in, I invite you on a journey to anchor yourself to the God who doesn't change when everything else is changing, to discover rhythms that help you find your footing, and to learn how to give yourself grace when you need it most. And hey, maybe after we journey together with courage through our seasons, we'll enter that sweet Season of Blooming after all. No promises.

Chapter 1

YOUR PRAYER WAS ANSWERED—NOW WHAT?

We perceive change as a threat, even if it is minor. We can also perceive change as a loss and if there is one thing our brain hates, it's the pain associated with loss.

—DR. MARC MILSTEIN AND BEN MOORSOM

Your prayer was answered—now what? Now you throw confetti, host a party, raise a glass for a toast, and tell all your friends. Now you snap a photo to document your miracle and post it on social media. Now you get to settle in and enjoy every moment of every day with your new blessing. You've arrived, right? Well, at least that's how it played out in your head. If you're anything like me, you've learned the hard way that the answer to a prayer is less of an arrival point and more like a starting line. Now it's time to build in the natural what you prayed for in the spiritual. Now it's time to step into a new season, enlarge your capacity, and adapt to change. Now is the time to navigate curveballs, untangle mixed emotions, and grieve losses. *This is what you prayed for, right?*

I thought I was the adventurous type—the one who prays big prayers and courageously steps into God's plans. Then the answer to my prayers arrived; I moved across the country for an exciting job opportunity and completed my family through adoption like I dreamed of. They were all good changes, and I was celebrating and grateful. But I simultaneously experienced unexpected grief and feelings of inadequacy, guilt, and confusion.

Do any of those sound familiar?

I watched my new children adjust to a new school, family, and neighborhood, and change wasn't easy for them either. The years I spent praying for my kids, they spent praying for a family. We all wanted the change, we prayed for it, and we chose it. But change is a funny thing. Even positive changes that we handpick and prepare for can blindside us with their emotional weight. My daughter said, "I thought I would be happy after I got adopted, and I am . . . but the emotions and the tears, they just come. I don't know how or why, but sometimes they just come."

Yes, sweet girl. They certainly do.

SWIMMING IN THE DARK

I took a scuba-diving class in college, and I'm ashamed to admit I passed the class without ever getting in the water. I guess all the preparation for what could go wrong got stuck in my head, and I couldn't move past the textbook. *My teeth could explode? What?! I'm good. Thanks.* The scariest thing I heard was that it's possible to get vertigo to the point where you don't know which way is up and which way is down. That imagery terrified me: swimming around frantically in blackness, blindly guessing which direction to swim in order to survive. What if you swim in the wrong direction? What if you pick a path, but it leads you farther into darkness? That imagery isn't far from how I've felt adjusting to the vertigo of too much change too fast in my real life.

Shortly after my family and I moved to Florida, we knew it didn't feel like home. No big deal. People move all the time, and not every move is a forever move. But the feeling of displacement was unlike anything I'd ever experienced (and I've moved a lot). Florida seemed like a different planet compared to where I grew up in the Pacific Northwest. I felt like I went scuba diving and swam in the wrong direction in the dark. I couldn't find my way back to the surface. I kept waking up thinking, *What have I done? Which way is forward?*

Florida is beautiful, and my job was a blessing. I prayed circles around the opportunity and experienced many confirmations that it was the right decision. So why did I keep waking up with a tightness in my chest and regret pulsing through my veins? Was it normal to experience this much shock to the system? Why did this particular move give me so much vertigo?

A couple of years in, things were starting to get a little better. I learned the optimal times to avoid getting eaten by bugs; I learned not to drink my coffee outside; I became familiar with toll roads and which ditches housed gators. The tightness in my chest didn't completely subside, but it started to wane into a dull ache. My husband and I were in the middle of the adoption process, so we agreed to wait until that was settled before we'd consider moving again. My husband was adopted at birth, and I was unconventionally adopted when I was taken in by my best friend's family as a teen. We had three biological children and decided we would adopt our fourth. We applied to adopt internationally, but after five years of waiting for a match, we were about to give up on the idea. Every day for five years, I prayed for that child. And every day I wondered if they were praying for a family too. Just as we were about to give up, I got a text from a parent at my kids' school. It said, "I just heard about a local sibling set in foster care who is in need of a forever family." Little did she know that text would change my life and the lives of those kids forever.

I had five years to imagine what adopting a child would be like. Five years' worth of expectations turned into the idea that I would transform into a cross between Mother Teresa and Maria von Trapp from *The Sound of Music*. I would wake up each morning and nourish them with fresh organic smoothies. I would patiently read wholesome literature aloud each day. I would limit their screen time, take them on nature walks, and bake homemade zucchini bread. I would devote my days to their healing and development and discipleship. I had a great plan, all wrapped up with a bow. Adoption was our thing, so I expected to walk into it with an "I was made for this" confidence.

When the kids joined our family, our daughter was eleven and our son was seven. They were, and still are, an answer to prayer. On the first day at home, our daughter said, "I feel like I've known you guys my whole life. It feels like I was on a long trip, but now I'm home." We felt the same way. Even our grumpy dog loved them immediately, which was a small miracle. Though our love was strong, our first weeks together were far from *The Sound of Music*. All seven of us got extremely sick. I felt like a zombie, taking care of five sick children while recovering myself. My husband developed pneumonia and couldn't get out of bed. I was navigating virtual school to help our kids finish out the school year in 2021. It was chaos. I lost weight. I couldn't sleep. I paced in my bathroom in the middle of the night. I had panic attacks. I was swimming in the dark. I didn't feel like I was made for this; I felt in over my head. I was no supermom; I was hot-mess mom—fully equipped with mystery stains and sprains, a cracked phone, stretchy pants, a turd bun, migraine meds, and cold coffee. *But I prayed for this?*

We all know what it's like to sit across the table from someone who is there but not really there. Can you think of a time when you've been in this situation? You feel like you are talking to someone and their mind is somewhere else, a visible body with a checked-out soul. That is the last thing I wanted to give my new kids. But sadly I spent far too many days in survival mode after they arrived. I knew I wasn't at my best; I knew I wasn't connecting the way I wanted to connect. But showing up was all I had to give. I felt disoriented by all the changes: the new energy in my home, the endless doctors' and counseling appointments, the tutoring, and the constant visits from caseworkers. (We had three sets of caseworkers since the kids were from out of the county!)

In addition to adjusting to the new family dynamics, I was still adjusting to life in Florida, and about a month before the adoption was final, I transitioned to another new job. I remember standing in front of the mirror saying, *I don't know how to get dressed anymore.* My previous role was (mostly) remote, so it had been over a decade since I worked full-time in an office. I bought far too many blouses, and everyone in my new office was so young that most of them had never heard of the word *blouse*. (*Great. Already killing it.*) On my morning commute I would thank God for it all, but I still felt out of place in my own life, like a foreigner trying to find my way back home.

After seven months of fostering (Florida law requires a period of fostering before you can adopt from foster care), my husband and I raised our hands before a judge and promised to love and care for our two new children. After countless delays, setbacks, and turnabouts, we were officially a forever family—now a party of seven. When the judge made the official announcement, our daughter ran over to hug us with tears streaming down her face and said, "You're my *mom*! And you're my *dad*!" This was indeed the finish line we'd all waited for, and I can't imagine a more fulfilling calling. So why didn't I feel *only* excitement and joy? Why did I also still feel inadequate, overwhelmed, and disoriented? My life felt like a snow globe that had been wildly shaken; I knew it was beautiful, but I couldn't see through all the unsettled fragments yet.

Around the same time, my friend's husband returned from deployment in Yemen. So to make myself feel better, I started going around saying to myself, *At least I'm not in Yemen*. Surely thinking of someone more displaced than me would flip the switch on my feelings. My little catchphrase didn't change my inner world much, but it did put a smile on my face on the tough days (*Yemen* is a fun word to say).

I wonder how many of us are living in survival mode, but we never talk about it. When people ask, "How are you?" I have yet to hear anyone say, "Well, I'm just surviving right now. How about you?" or "I feel like I'm swimming in the dark and my teeth might explode. How's your week going?" I wonder if sometimes we don't even realize we're just surviving, merely sleepwalking. How long has it been since we felt like ourselves?

When our nervous systems are dysregulated and stressed, we are unable to activate the parts of the brain that help us feel grounded. You know, the parts that make you feel like *you*. It's difficult to connect with others or have a clear perspective, because our bodies are trying to survive. I've been through capital *T* traumatic events in my life, like my mom's sudden and tragic death when I was sixteen. So I felt confused when these *good* changes in my life sent me into a tailspin of dysregulation and survival mode more than any other time in my life.

The Holmes and Rahe stress scale was developed by psychiatrists Thomas Holmes and Richard Rahe in 1967 to rank life events based on the level of stress they typically cause. The Holmes–Rahe study found that accumulating high-stress life events within a short period increases the likelihood of illness. If someone's total score exceeds 300 life change units (LCUs) in a year, they have a high risk of developing health problems due to stress.[1] The top stressors on the list are the death of a spouse, a divorce or separation from a spouse, and imprisonment—all traumatic events, no doubt about it. But do you know what's also on the list of stressful life events? Pregnancy, gaining a new family member, switching jobs, moving, starting or finishing school, a change in church activities or recreation, and even an outstanding personal achievement. Here are some transitions you may relate to and their LCUs.

- Getting married: 50 LCUs
- Pregnancy: 40 LCUs
- Gaining a new family member (birth, adoption, remarriage, etc.): 39 LCUs
- Major business adjustment (or major changes at work): 39 LCUs

- Change in financial state (better or worse): 38 LCUs
- Changing to a different line of work: 36 LCUs
- Outstanding personal achievement (major success in career, academics, or personal life): 28 LCUs
- Spouse starts or stops work: 26 LCUs
- Beginning or finishing school: 26 LCUs
- Change in living conditions (renovations, lifestyle shifts): 25 LCUs
- Change in personal habits (health, diet, routines): 24 LCUs
- Change in residence (moving to a new home): 20 LCUs
- Change in recreation (new hobbies, interests, lifestyle changes): 19 LCUs
- Change in church activities (more involvement, leadership, stepping back, etc.): 19 LCUs
- Change in social activities (new friendships, social circles, commitments): 18 LCUs
- Christmas or a major holiday season: 12 LCUs

These are only some of the positive changes that cause stress in our bodies. And some life changes accumulate more LCUs by nature. For someone like me who moved across the country with their family, they could experience 100-plus LCUs after combining the housing, social, work, and lifestyle shifts, making it a significant life stressor even though it's a positive change. And for me, adding two new family members and changing jobs only increased that LCU total.

There is a difference between eustress and distress. Eustress is a positive form of stress that can motivate, challenge, and help you grow rather than overwhelm you. It's the kind of stress that pushes you out of your comfort zone but in a way that's manageable and beneficial. Eustress can become distress when it's layered with too much change or pressure or a lack of rest. You can tell your body, *Don't worry. This is good stress.* But depending on how much change and pressure you're experiencing (or lack of rest), your body can struggle to parse out the stress coming from something good and positive. It only knows that it's stressed, and it responds accordingly. Additionally, big life changes can cause our bodies to surface buried trauma or grief. Like a dormant autoimmune disease that is suddenly activated, unprocessed trauma can resurface during a big life change, even a positive one. (Inconvenient timing, I know. I'll share more about this in a later chapter.) I'm not saying this as a therapist or an expert; I'm saying this as someone who experienced such unexpected confusion, a shock to the system, and a survival-mode response that I had to figure out what the heck was going on. I was the patient, not the doctor.

We often minimize our feelings or dismiss our survival mode as "I've just been tired lately." We try to brush off the confusion, or we feel too proud to admit we have spiritual vertigo and need help. It's powerful when we can acknowledge that we are swimming in the dark, trying to survive. But instead we bottle up our feelings and hit ourselves over the head with this statement: "But I prayed for this." We assume that if we tell anyone how much we're struggling, we'll get the same response from them.

"Well, this is what you prayed for."

"This is what you wanted."

"You chose this."

These scenarios, real or assumed, only dig our graves of guilt deeper. And it's all true. But can we still admit it's hard? Is there a safe place we can go when we are both celebrating and struggling?

Is there a place for those in a Season of Building to acknowledge they are both grateful and grinding?

Is there a place for those in a Bittersweet Season to confess that it's hard to hold a dream in one hand and disappointment in the other?

Is there a place for those in a Season of Balancing to admit their emotions don't align with their circumstances?

When my best friend called to ask how I was doing, I jumped to a quick summary about the kids, assuming that's what she wanted to hear. I told her how our daughter broke down crying and told us her whole life story in what seemed like one breath. At the end of it, she said, "But I wouldn't change it, because it led me here to you guys, and this feels like where I belong." I shared with my friend how we finally got my new son to eat more than just grapes and how he was doing great in swimming lessons. I summed it all up with positivity, because sometimes I do that without thinking. But there's something about a friend who knows you well enough to see beyond the surface. She said, "How are you *really* doing? Tell me about the hard."

It takes a big person to hold space for someone else's hard. That day, she gave me permission to say it out loud: I was only surviving. I was fully submerged and disoriented. I was swimming in a new season, and I couldn't find my sense of direction yet. There was gratitude and excitement and joy, but also there was trauma to wade through and change to adjust to. Even with years of preparation, most days I felt unprepared and unqualified to handle it all. I wasn't the gold-star mom I wanted to be, but I was a mom who would keep showing up—gold, silver, bronze, or rusty (I've mostly been rusty). My friend didn't fix my problems; she couldn't. But she said, "I'm so proud of you. You're doing so well." And she reminded me of a God who is the same yesterday, today, and forever.* I didn't feel

* Hebrews 13:8.

like I was doing "so well," and she wasn't telling me anything about God I didn't already know. But when you're drowning in darkness, the simplest words of truth can feel like someone is at the surface shining a light that reminds you which direction to swim.

Shauna Niequist said, "We sometimes choose the most locked up, dark versions of the story, but what a good friend does is turn on the lights, open the window, and remind us that there are a whole lot of ways to tell the same story."[2] I hope to be that friend for you in this book. I might not tell you anything you don't already know. The truth I share might not be profound, revelatory, or new. But no one complains about a little oxygen when they're drowning or a little light when it's pitch-black.

Here's what I want you to know: You have permission to be in survival mode, but God won't keep you there. Survival mode is a necessary reality at times, but it's not sustainable. When we are swimming in circles with spiritual vertigo, God wants to be our stable reference point—the light we follow back to the surface.

I'm sure you've heard phrases like "Stop surviving and start thriving." While I agree that thriving is the aim, I've also come to realize that there's a place for surviving. Telling someone to hurry up and thrive is like telling a seed to hurry up and sprout. It will. It just needs the right elements and some time. A surviving seed is a seed that's still alive, and the fact that it's alive means it's slowly working its way toward growth. It's germinating in the dark. And maybe if God does that with seeds, he does that with us too. Swimming in the dark might be uncomfortable, but what if the depths of darkness teach us to reorient ourselves toward the light? What if the seasons we feel buried beneath the surface are the very thing God uses to prepare us for rebirth?

I won't prod you to move faster through survival mode, but I can help you find the right direction in the darkness. Let's make our way back to the "Father of heavenly lights, who does not change like shifting shadows."* And on our darkest and most breathless days, let's take a moment to remind ourselves that at least we're not in Yemen.

CHANGE FATIGUE

Change fatigue is a term commonly used to describe the employees of an organization who experience one change after another.[3] Employees experience physical, emotional, and mental exhaustion when they're asked to continually adapt to new changes, especially when those changes are frequent, overwhelming, or not well managed. When another initiative is thrown their way, they may start to feel cynical or wonder, *What's the point?* (because another change is going to come again anyway). I think personal change fatigue is just as valid as professional fatigue. As we try to adapt to cumulative life changes, we sometimes don't realize how much we slide into fatigue and resignation.

I asked some friends to tell me the funniest thing they've ever done when they were tired. A few of my favorites were

- "I waited for a stop sign to turn green."
- "I tried to find my phone while I was using it."
- "I put a baby bottle under the Keurig instead of a coffee cup."
- "My husband put the pacifier in my mouth instead of the baby's."

* James 1:17.

- "I answered a phone call from my boss with 'Hi, honey!'"
- "I scooped dog food into the coffee maker thinking it was coffee grounds."
- "I woke up, got the baby and myself ready, got in the car, and started driving. Fifteen minutes in I realized I had no idea where I was going and had nowhere to be. So I turned around and went back to bed."

Humor aside, we know we aren't at our best when we're tired. We say things we don't mean, complain about things we usually love, and feel unmotivated. Tonight, two out of my five children are hyperemotional and irrational because they just need sleep. But of course, when they're little they exclaim through the tears and bags under their eyes, "I'm not tired!"

There's the kind of tired that sleep can solve, but some seasons bring soul-level weariness. I once heard about a guy who moved across the country and slept twelve to fourteen hours every night for the first ten months. I thought it was unusual until the same thing happened to my husband after we moved to Florida.

A few months before the adoption was finalized, I flew to Texas for the weekend to visit one of my best friends, Jenny. It was the first time in months that I didn't have anyone else to take care of—let alone the first time I had a moment to myself to process my new family and new life—but all I could do was sleep. I slept an embarrassing number of hours on that trip. I kept telling Jenny, "I promise I came here to see you. Not sleep!" But I couldn't help it; my body crashed.

As we adapt to the changes around us, we can experience stress, fear, and exhaustion. The tangled web of emotions and thoughts might cause us to question if we made the right choice or if we're in

God's will. But what if our bodies just experienced a bout of change fatigue at an inconvenient time?

My youngest daughter came into my bedroom during that season and said, "Mom, I feel like crying for no reason again." At first I chalked it up to tweenage hormones, but over time I realized she wasn't crying for no reason. She was crying because change is tiring.

No amount of sleep or spa days can resolve soul-level weariness. It's a different kind of tired. To make matters worse, we reach for distractions. It's hard to argue with the statistics: The average internet user spends two hours and twenty-seven minutes daily on social media, and the average American spends over three hours watching television.[4] It's a catch-22: We're too tired to connect, pray, honor our emotions, or make healthy choices, so we zone out for a while and do it all over again the next day.

In addition to exhaustion and zoning out with distractions, you might recognize other symptoms of change fatigue: cynicism, a desire to quit, disorientation, brain fog, doubts about your capability, smaller capacity, shorter fuse, lower social battery, and perhaps feelings of guilt that you aren't carrying it all with ease. Personal change fatigue can't be diagnosed, and I'm guessing if you brought up the term to your doctor, they might tilt their head in confusion. But I speak as someone who experienced it for myself and have spoken with many others who felt the same—we weren't depressed or hopeless; we were recalibrating.

What does it take for us to admit we have change fatigue? What does it look like to recognize we are in a vulnerable season of change and to stop trying to cover it up with Band-Aids of distraction? Our bodies may certainly require extra sleep. But when we are soul-level weary, it's not only our bodies that need care; it's also our souls. And if the solution for our souls isn't a spa day or Netflix, what is it?

Jesus didn't offer a twelve-step solution; he offered himself. In Matthew 11:28–30 he said, "Come to me, all who labor and are heavy laden, and I will give you rest. Take my yoke upon you, and learn from me, for I am gentle and lowly in heart, and you will find rest for your souls. For my yoke is easy, and my burden is light" (ESV).

Eugene Peterson's paraphrase in *The Message* says it this way: "Are you tired? Worn out? Burned out on religion? Come to me. Get away with me and you'll recover your life. I'll show you how to take a real rest. Walk with me and work with me—watch how I do it. Learn the unforced rhythms of grace. I won't lay anything heavy or ill-fitting on you. Keep company with me and you'll learn to live freely and lightly."

Jesus made some pretty big promises: recover our lives, discover how to take a real rest, learn the unforced rhythms of grace, and learn to live lightly and freely. Where do I sign up? What product or method or program can deliver this? Because Netflix isn't working.

What if the answer to the weariness of our souls isn't found in a method but in a Messiah? Not in a program but in a Person. What if the light way of living is found in connection to the Light? Will he take us as we are—in a battered state of survival mode and change fatigue? The answer is yes. The invitation is open even on the days when we're waiting for the stop sign to turn green.

DIRECTION WHEN YOU'RE DROWNING

In the last chapter of his book *Stolen Focus*, Johann Hari shared what he learned from former Google strategist James Williams about the three types of attention. He labeled them *spotlight*, *starlight*, and *daylight*. Here's a short breakdown of the three:

1. **Spotlight** involves the attention needed for immediate actions, like walking into the kitchen to grab your coffee. This involves narrowing down your focus for short-term actions.
2. **Starlight** involves the type of focus you need for longer-term goals, such as starting a business or being a good parent. If you become distracted from your starlight, you forget your long-term goals and where you're headed.
3. **Daylight** makes it possible to know the *why* around your long-term goals. This requires the ability to reflect and think clearly. If you lose daylight focus, you don't have the mental space to form a story about who you are or where you're headed.[5]

When I read about the different types of focus, I immediately thought of the connection between change fatigue and focus. We lack the mental and emotional margin for starlight or daylight when our bodies are overloaded, and we have the capacity for only spotlight (you know, the essentials, like walking to and from the coffee maker). When you are finding your footing and establishing a new norm, it's easy to forget the story of who you are and where you're headed. And as believers we've been invited into the best story—God's story. It's a story of redemption and healing, a story of eternity and new life; it's a story full of purpose and meaning and supernatural power. And yet even the best story gets foggy when our minds, bodies, and souls are in a season of recalibration.

My season of change literally scared the daylight out of me, which is why my friend's reminders of simple truths meant so much. I needed to remember that God is good, I'm a good mom, and my feelings wouldn't last forever. I needed to remember why

I moved to Florida, why I stepped into my new job, and why I believed (and still do) in caring for kids from hard places. Those simple truths pointed me toward the surface when I didn't know which direction to swim.

When I was having panic attacks, a therapist told me the first order of business was to get those under control. He told me the next time a panic attack hit, he wanted me to look around the room and begin naming everything I saw.

Desk.

Chair.

Lamp.

Painting.

Pillow.

What kind of preschool assignment was this? My therapist explained that when we are dysregulated, we need something that helps bring us back to the present moment. Our minds don't want complex information; they want to be grounded again. When I look back on the times I've struggled the most, it's not the big revelations, epiphanies, or insights that I've lost sight of; it's the basics. Losing sight of the simple truths (or losing faith in the simple truths) is often what's tripped me up the most. Eventually I rediscover basic truths again, such as "God holds my future," "God is my source for joy and strength," and "My feelings aren't final." And I give myself a good facepalm for forgetting.

When you're swimming in the dark, you don't need someone to throw you a textbook on scuba diving; you need someone to point to the surface so you can come up for air. What basics do you need to remember? What simple truths are in front of you right now? What story have you lost sight of?

You are loved.

There's no need to strive.
You are not your feelings.
God's got this.

Pray It Through

God, thank you that you invite me to be honest about where I am. I admit that I sometimes feel like I'm swimming in the dark. Help me find my way back to the light. Thank you for my answer to prayer. Thank you that you understand the complexity of change fatigue and mixed emotions, and you invite me to anchor my soul in you, the God who is the same yesterday, today, and forever. Amen.

Anchor Your Soul

If your season of change has left you feeling out of sorts, here are a few questions to help you find your way back to the light.

1. Which season do you find yourself in?
    - A Season of Blooming (Everything is smooth; I'm reading this book for fun.)
    - A Season of Building (more work than expected)
    - A Bittersweet Season (navigating grief and gratitude simultaneously)
    - A Season of Balancing (mismatched and/or unexpected emotions)

2. Which type of focus do you need restored the most?
    - Spotlight: immediate day-to-day actions
    - Starlight: long-term focus and goals
    - Daylight: your *why* and the bigger story of your life
    - All of the above
3. What is one small thing you can do daily that helps you feel clearheaded?
4. What is your *why*? (Write it down.)
5. Who is one person you can call to remind you of simple truths?

Chapter 2

WHAT DID YOU EXPECT?

It's not the hard roads that slay us; what actually slays us is the expectation that this road isn't what we hoped it to be.

—ANN VOSKAMP

Expectations. That one little word that carries so much weight. The funny thing about expectations is that we often don't know they exist until they aren't met. I never spoke my expectations aloud about how I would feel after I moved, adopted, or started my new job. I never wrote them down in a journal or uttered my expectations in a prayer. They were just there—unspoken expectations and assumptions about how good changes in life were supposed to feel.

So I have a question for you (and I don't mean it in a sassy way): What did you expect? Like me, did you expect your answer to prayer to feel different or your life to be easier? Did you expect it to come as an undiluted blessing without any curveballs or trials? Did you expect to feel confident, but instead you felt clumsy?

Expectations are unavoidable. From our upbringing to what we see in the movies to the sermons we hear at church on Sundays, we all unknowingly store up narratives about how life is supposed to go, how things are supposed to feel, or how God is supposed to act. What makes it harder for believers in Jesus is that we are called to have faith, and faith and expectations can become a tangled mess if left unchecked.

Remember the prayer of Jabez I mentioned in the introduction? Jabez prayed for God to bless him, enlarge his territory, and give him a harm-free, pain-free life. "God granted his request."* That's it. It was that simple. I'm happy for Jabez, because that's what I pray over my children. I want them to be blessed and protected from harm and pain. Full stop. But I also recognize that God's story for Jabez doesn't make it a formula for all humanity. It doesn't mean persistent prayers or good behavior will automatically grant us mess-free, fairy-tale endings that lead to a Season of Blooming.

We are called to have faith in God, his power, his goodness, and his promises, but when we slip into specific expectations, sometimes that can get sticky. The problem isn't that we can't have expectations; the problem is that we need an adjustment in what we expect. And we need to figure out where we went off course.

In this chapter I'm going to help you adjust your expectations and identify where you may have picked up a faulty expectation along the way. I'm also going to help you expect the right things and center your heart to welcome God's goodness in ways that don't

---

* 1 Chronicles 4:10.

leave you so disillusioned. Adjusting our expectations doesn't solve everything, but it does help us sort through the mental clutter so we don't just *go* through our transition; we *grow* through it.

REWARD PREDICTION ERROR

My adoptive mom (a.k.a. Nanny) flew in over Mother's Day weekend to help me. It was my first break from all the kids, my first time coming up for air after the whirlwind of placement, virtual school, and brain fog. And I could not wait to spend the day at a spa with my mom—nothing sounded better. As elated as I was to get a respite, the dam of my emotions broke when we were driving to the resort. Tears burst out of my eyes, blurring my vision so much that I nearly had to pull over. I spoke out loud my most desperate thought, "I don't think I can do this. I really don't think I can do it."

I was afraid that I didn't have what it took to help my new children heal and that I would never adjust to life in Florida or my new job. I was afraid of who I'd become: someone who couldn't find her bearings, who felt disoriented and disillusioned. I'm usually the one who has a plan, the eternal optimist, the resilient one who never shrinks from a challenge or change. So why were all these good changes pulling me under?

Nanny said, "You can do it, and you will. You always find a way. Things will get easier, and you will feel like yourself again. Just take it one day at a time."

With tears smeared across my face, I took a deep breath. Nanny's words weighed a thousand pounds. She'd traveled down this road before, embracing me as a traumatized fourteen-year-old girl and standing with me through my messy process toward healing. Her daughter, Brittany, was my best friend in high school. Their home became a refuge for me when things got chaotic in my own. Eventually, when it was no longer safe for me to stay with my biological mom, Nanny took me in. The adoption was never official on paper, but it became official in our hearts. And it was always my *why* for adopting—to give a child what someone gave me.

Nanny was right—I needed to take it one day at a time—and she was gracious with my meltdown. But my uncontrollable waterworks were so unlike me that I shocked even myself. I wondered, *Why does it feel like I fell so far so fast? Why do I feel so low when my life is supposed to be on a high?*

It turns out this kind of disillusionment isn't just emotional; it's physiological.

Dopamine is the brain chemical released during positive life experiences. It's often called the pleasure or anticipation chemical. Dopamine doesn't just react to what happens; it also responds to what we *expect* to happen. Our brains start predicting what we'll want or need, and as those expectations build, our dopamine levels rise, sometimes long before we reach the milestone. (Ever felt a rush of excitement just thinking about something good that's coming? That's your dopamine throwing a party with your expectations.) When things turn out the way we hoped, we get a double dose of dopamine: first from anticipation, then from fulfillment. Major party. But when reality doesn't meet our expectations, it creates what neuroscientists call a "reward prediction error." In other words, your brain expected a payoff and didn't get it. So not only do your dopamine levels drop; they fall from the height of your expectations. The higher and more specific the expectation, the harder the crash. Instead of a double dose of joy, you get a double dose of disillusionment.[1]

As for me and those first weeks with my new kids, I expected *The Sound of Music*, which is a pretty tall order. But the reality? My life felt like the movie *Twister*—a tornado of sickness, insomnia, mixed emotions, virtual school, visits from social workers, panic attacks, brain fog, and the pressure to give my best when I felt like my worst. It was one strange reward prediction error that I felt guilty about, because that was what I had prayed for.

Maybe you can relate. The marriage, the baby, the job, the ministry—it was the cry of your heart, and God answered. So is it selfish or ungrateful to feel disillusioned? Or did your answer to prayer come with a reward prediction error (and change fatigue) that your body is still adjusting to? You're fulfilled, but you're also frustrated. The reality of your answered prayer came with a helping of heaviness that you didn't see coming. You expected a Season of Blooming, but you're left in a Bittersweet Season or a Season of Building or Balancing. This gap between what you expected and your experience can shake your confidence in God and in yourself.

Did I mishear God?

Are gifts from God supposed to be this hard?

Is something wrong with me?

John Maxwell said, "Disappointment is the gap that exists between expectation and reality."[2] Which is why I asked you, "What did you expect?" Not because I'm shaking my finger at you saying, "It's all your fault"—quite the opposite. Like a crime scene investigator, I want to help you examine the wall of expectations you came tumbling down from, because naming those unspoken expectations can help your brain examine what led to your reward prediction error.

Chances are you've experienced reward prediction errors in small ways your whole life. When I was a newlywed, I was quite the prankster. It was Thanksgiving and we lived in Las Vegas at the time. Since my aunt was in town visiting, she invited us to a fancy restaurant for Thanksgiving—her treat. The restaurant was in one of the hotels known for being cool, posh, modern, and sleek. Not exactly the usual Thanksgiving scene, but my husband and I weren't paying for dinner and didn't have to cook, and we've always been up for new experiences. When we entered the building, my husband leaned over and whispered in my ear, "I really hope this isn't one of those fancy places that serves you tiny portions." After all, it was Thanksgiving, the one day a year everyone wears stretchy pants for a reason.

I said, "Oh, I wouldn't worry about that. It's Thanksgiving. I'm sure they are prepared with a buffet or something."

The restaurant was a dimly lit room with blue neon lights under the bar area. The tables were made of gray stone, and the floors were concrete. After our server introduced himself, I slipped out to go to the restroom. On my way back I pulled our server aside. I said, "Hey, I was hoping to play a little joke on my husband. He's nervous about the portions being small. No matter what he orders, can you bring out a tiny portion at first?" Surprisingly, the server agreed. All our plates (besides his) arrived loaded to the edges with a Thanksgiving feast. But when the server put my husband's plate in front of him, it beautifully showcased one baby carrot, a slice of meat the size of my thumb, a couple of garnishes, and a drizzle of sauce. My husband's face turned bright red. He leaned over to me and said, "What did I order?"

We all had a good laugh, and they finally brought out his real plate, full to the edge with delicious food like all the others. But I'll never forget the reward prediction error reflected on his flushed red face when he expected a Thanksgiving feast but received a toddler's snack.

Sometimes what's on your plate when it arrives is not what you expected. But other times, your reward prediction error is less about what's on your plate and more about how you *feel* when it arrives. In the book of Exodus, it seems like Moses would have felt honored and excited to be chosen as Israel's leader to the promised land. Instead he kept pointing out his shortcomings to God and felt like God picked the wrong person for the job.* (Moses and I would have been fast friends.) Because Moses didn't feel how a leader "should" feel—confident and capable—he doubted God's calling. He assumed his stutter disqualified him from being the best person for the job. Moses was in a Season of Balancing, and he had to learn how to carry his calling even when his feelings weren't falling in line.

When I examined my own reward prediction error, I realized one of the problems with my expectations was that I didn't feel in control anymore. I missed knowing what to expect each day, and I missed feeling competent and in charge. I expected to feel confident as I stepped into God's plans, but instead I felt dependent, like a baby learning to walk, reaching frantically for stability. It's easy to say Jesus is Lord of our lives but hard to put it into practice when we are forced to trade our self-reliance for God-reliance during seasons of intense change. The truth is, control is an illusion. There is only one who controls the winds and the waves, and it's Jesus, not us.† And even though we know we are supposed to live in daily dependence on God, it's the seasons that stretch us out of our comfort zones that put our dependence to the test.

God uses change fatigue and reward prediction errors to help us to adjust our expectations, reorder our lives, and learn the power

---

* Exodus 4:10–17.

† Matthew 8:27.

of depending on God's strength and not our own. God spoke to the apostle Paul, saying, "My grace is sufficient for you, for my power is made perfect in weakness."* Paul was surrounded by those who wanted to be seen as superapostles, boasting about their pedigree and accomplishments, but he flipped the script and boasted about his weakness and dependence on God instead. We usually expect seasons of crisis and tragedy to make us come to the end of ourselves, so it's surprising to feel desperate when we get everything we prayed for. But it's not always the valleys where we learn to depend on God the most; sometimes it's the mountaintops. And it takes courage to admit that even though we've reached a peak in life, we aren't standing tall; we are bowing low.

RACHAEL'S SEASON OF BUILDING

Have you ever had one of these thoughts?

> *Maybe I'm too old.*
> *Maybe I'm not capable.*
> *Maybe it's too late.*

One of my sisters, Rachael, wrestled with the idea of pursuing her dream to go back to school to become a certified registered nurse anesthesiologist (CRNA). She'd been a bedside nurse for six years and heard stories about how rigorous the CRNA program was. Not to mention Rachael wasn't even sure if she'd get into the program. She dreamed of attending Georgetown University, a

* 2 Corinthians 12:9–10.

top-ten school with its own cadaver lab and a reputation for having med-school-level education. But she knew the odds were stacked against her. She was a mom with a family and would be the oldest in her class. Would she be able to juggle it all?

Despite her doubts, Rachael prayed about it. *God, show me if this is what I'm supposed to do,* she whispered one night.

The next day she went out to check the mail. It was a stack of junk mail, but one envelope caught her eye. The envelope had a fake loan application in it, with a little card attached that said "Certified Registered Nurse Anesthesiologist" beneath her name. It felt like a wink from God. Who else knew about this specific dream but him? That little piece of junk mail became a treasure. Rachael tucked it into her wallet and started the application process.

Rachael still had her doubts, but the day she received the email from Georgetown was one of the best days of her life. When she read the words "Congratulations! You've been accepted!" she collapsed on the floor sobbing. "I got in! I got in!" she said through breathless tears. It was an answer to prayer, a dream come true, and a gift from God. Only it wasn't the finish line; it was the starting line.

Rachael expected it to be hard, but she had no idea how hard. The first year was an overwhelming blur of intense classes and exams, followed by two years of clinical residencies that demanded forty to seventy hours of her time a week and were never in the same hospital (with more classes, studying, and researching on top). Days began before dawn with safety checks and patient assessments, then stretched late into the night with case logs and studying. The grueling pace left little time for family, and with every missed dinner, birthday, or sporting event, her mom guilt grew heavier. No matter how much she gave, she felt like she was either failing at school or failing at home.

There were many times Rachael wanted to quit. She found herself regularly having panic attacks and frequenting her program director's office in tears. She learned that among anesthesiology trainees, there was a high prevalence of burnout, drug diversion, depression, and suicidal ideation.[3] She did not want to become one of the statistics. But she didn't feel like she could open up to people about how hard it was. She feared they would remind her of what she already knew: This was what she wanted, this was what she chose, and this was what she prayed for.

One breathless day in her director's office, her director said to her, "Rachael, we chose you for a reason. You are capable. Keep going." Around that time she overheard her son talking to a friend about how proud he was of his mom. It was all she needed to put a fresh wind in her sails. She pulled the junk-mail card out of her wallet as a reminder of her wink from God and remembered the moment when she felt called.

Despite underestimating how rigorous the program would be, the continued mom guilt, and all the days she wanted to quit, Rachael completed the CRNA program and sat in her director's office one last time for her exit interview. The director said, "I'm proud of you, and I would trust you to give anesthesia to my own children. You're one of the most resilient students we've ever had in the program."

Rachael hung the wallet-sized wink from God right next to her diploma. She loves her job, caring for patients and being a comforting presence when they're nervous before surgery or groggy after. But she can't deny that although it was worth it, those three years were some of the hardest years of her life. Georgetown was an answer to prayer, but it was an answer that kept her on her knees in daily dependence.

MORE RUBBLE THAN EXPECTED

In the book of Nehemiah, we read about a man named Nehemiah, who was the cupbearer to the Persian king. When Nehemiah heard that Jerusalem's walls had been destroyed, the news broke his heart. He wept, fasted, and prayed desperately for days. And he specifically asked God for an opportunity to speak to the king about it: "O Lord, please hear my prayer! Listen to the prayers of those of us who delight in honoring you. Please grant me success today by making the king favorable to me. Put it into his heart to be kind to me."*

Nehemiah's prayer was answered, and the king granted him a leave of absence so he could rebuild the walls. Nehemiah was confident God would help his plan succeed, and he rallied people to begin the rebuilding process. But the God-given mission wasn't without opposition. Nehemiah and the workers were mocked and threatened. People said, "Do they actually think they can make something of stones from a rubbish heap?"†

The mocks and threats weren't the only challenge; the workers were growing tired because there was so much rubble to move, and they were struggling to feed their families. They worked early and late, from sunrise to sunset. And because of all the threats they received, they each held a weapon to defend themselves in one hand and a tool to build in the other.

At the end of the book of Nehemiah, even the workers' enemies recognized that God was with them in their work. The wall was rebuilt, and Nehemiah led people in a time of spiritual renewal. But most of the book is about the messy middle—the hardship of

* Nehemiah 1:11 NLT.
† Nehemiah 4:2 NLT.

moving so much rubble, facing opposition, and pushing through when they had every reason to quit.

Seasons of Building are a lot like those long days Nehemiah and his workers spent trying to build something from rubble. Even when you know your assignment is from God, sometimes there's more rubble than expected. And though you may not face literal mockers, you face the same doubts: Will my work really be worth it? Can I really make something of all this rubble?

Doubt can lead to discouragement, and discouragement leads to weariness. There's a misconception that when you are in God's will, you will always feel peaceful and the grace of God will preclude you from hard work. Just because you have God's yes and his grace doesn't mean life will always feel easy or smooth or that it will come without a fight. Even though it's a God-given assignment, a Season of Building can be tiring. But being at the point of exhaustion in your calling doesn't mean you're doing it wrong; you're just at the point when most people quit. In those moments God doesn't redirect us to a different calling, but he does teach us how to carry our callings differently. And those lessons are the gems we never forget—lessons that are embedded so deeply they become a part of who we are. My sister didn't just learn about persistence in her CRNA program; she became persistent. She didn't just learn about resilience; she became resilient. She didn't just say, "I depend on God's strength daily"; she lived it.

Even though they were tired, Nehemiah and his crew didn't give up; they learned how to hold a weapon for defense in one hand and a tool for building in the other. And we can learn something from this strategy. Seasons of Building require us to hold our work in one hand and our weapon of worship in the other. We are grateful, but we're also grinding. We can't expect Seasons of Building to come free from trouble or tenacity, so it begs the question, What can we expect?

WHAT TO EXPECT WHEN YOU'RE EXPECTING

What to expect when you're expecting—no, I don't mean the book about pregnancy. I mean, What *should* we expect when our brains were designed to expect something? What can we expect that doesn't set us up for reward prediction errors and a double dose of disappointment or discouragement?

God wants us to have faith. The Scriptures are clear about this. But God doesn't promise that he'll work according to our timelines, or that he'll reward us with the right feelings, or that blessings will arrive with ease. God promises his faithfulness, his presence, his strength, his forgiveness, and his love—among other things—but he does not promise that we will always feel good about his blessings or that his plans won't come without challenges.

I'm learning, slowly but surely, that life is ever-changing and unpredictable. But I *can* predict, expect, and count on the faithfulness of God. That is one thing my brain was designed to latch on to. I can expect God's goodness and mercy to "follow me all the days of my life."* I can accept that his goodness and mercy will not always look the way I want them to, feel how I expected them to feel, or come to fruition on my timeline. I can expect God's loving-kindness and accept the reality that it will probably look different than I think it will. When my brain latches on to the goodness of God, it helps me remember that God works all things together for

* Psalm 23:6.

my good, even the things I don't understand.* It helps interrupt my inner dialogue that tries to interpret my circumstances or my emotions as punishment, a sign I did something wrong, or worse, a sign that I am wrong. Instead of getting caught up in judgmental labels, it helps me remember that no matter what, God has a plan and his faithfulness never ends.†

Many Eastern religions are about detachment, and there's an element of wisdom in that. But as believers in Christ, we can take it a step further. We can detach from outcomes while attaching fully to God. We can detach from the how, what, where, when, and why while fully clinging to the Who. We can release our expectations around timelines, feelings, and how smooth or bumpy the ride will be, while fully trusting that God will be present, near, and faithful through it all.‡

The word *disillusion* means the "loss of illusion." It's the feeling that comes from discovering that something you believed in or idolized is not exactly what you expected. It's the state of being freed from illusions or false ideas and is often replaced with a sense of disenchantment or disappointment. Disillusionment happens when God reveals our illusions and shows us that he exists outside of conforming to our expectations. Although painful, the best part of breaking free from disillusionment is that we get to see what's real, what's reliable, and what's unwavering. And when the dust settles, my friends, you will realize it was God all along.

He is our firm foundation, what we can predict, expect, and build our lives on. A sense of *dis*appointment (in ourselves or our circumstances) becomes an opportunity to *re*appoint our focus and

---

* Romans 8:28.

† Psalm 117:2.

‡ Psalm 145:18.

dependence back toward him and his trustworthy character. That is what to expect when you're expecting.

FALLING TIDE: EXPECT A GOOD CATCH

I grew up in the damp Pacific Northwest with avid fisherman and hunters on my dad's side of the family. As a young boy, my Grandpa Bob would sneak out of the house to fish in the nearby streams of Buxton, Oregon (though it could hardly be called sneaking, since his mother always knew). When he became a man, Grandpa Bob upgraded his fishing trips to the base of the Bonneville Dam, Ghost Hole in Garibaldi, or the Columbia River to catch salmon or sturgeon. I went with him only once or twice as a child. I don't remember if I caught anything, but I remember feeling like anything was possible with my line in the water and my grandpa by my side.

One thing I learned from Grandpa Bob is that one of the best times to catch fish is during a falling tide, when the tide is going out or transitioning. When the tide turns and falls, baitfish get stirred up and game fish feast on all the transported food. The moving water seems to flip on a feeding switch. Practically the only mistake you can make is not having your line in the water. If you put in your line, you'll pull fish out one after another. Slack tides, when the water is not transitioning, are often the worst times for fishing. Becoming a good fisherman is more about taking advantage of moving tides—rising or falling—than it is about finding the best watering holes. I can imagine my grandpa anticipating the turning tides in his camo coveralls, with his pole in one hand and his red Solo cup in the other.

Falling tide is one of the best times to show up, throw out a line, and anticipate a good catch. What if we saw life transitions more like falling tide? What if our lines of connection to God during transitions were the optimal time to catch what he wants to teach us?

Anyone can stand on the shoreline and witness fishermen taking advantage of falling tide, but it's another thing entirely to decide to participate yourself. And maybe that's the point: Tides will never stop turning. So the question is, How will you respond when they turn? Will you cling tightly to your expectations, or will you surrender to what God wants you to catch? Will you let your reward prediction error keep you stuck in disillusionment, or will you lean in and see what else God has in store?

Fishermen don't usually know exactly what kinds of fish they will catch or how big they will be. Part of the thrill of the catch is not knowing when the fish will bite. Fishermen have learned how to expect something *good* without knowing exactly what it will look like or when it will come.

It's no wonder Jesus called fishermen to be his followers. To the rest of society they seemed like the unlikely choice. They weren't polished, put together, or in a prestigious profession. They were salt-of-the-earth kind of men, like my grandpa, with dirt under their fingernails and calluses on their hands. They weren't the type of crowd who let disappointment hold them back. Fishermen know how to stand by the water for hours, casting their lines in for the hundredth time. They know how to wait, hope, trust, and persevere.

That's the problem with the falling-tide seasons of life: We don't see them as optimal times. Fishermen anticipate moving tides; they position themselves for the transitions. When everyone leans out, fishermen lean in. Fishermen anticipate what others tolerate.

They see what's possible beneath the surface—they see that the best catches are worth the wait.

Are you willing to wait to see what God wants to show you through your season of change? Are you willing to expect his goodness through your Seasons of Building or Balancing or your Bittersweet Season, even if it looks and feels different than you thought it would?

Jesus described the kingdom of heaven as "a net that was let down into the lake and caught all kinds of fish."* In Luke 5, at the Sea of Galilee, Jesus told Peter and the weary fishermen with him to let down their nets for a catch one more time, even though they had been fishing all night and came up empty-handed. They did what fishermen do: They tried again. With sore muscles, tired eyes, and salty hair, they cast again, this time catching so many fish that "their nets began to break" (v. 6). If the men had held a skeptical, been-there, done-that attitude, they would have passed on Jesus's prompting. What does a rabbi know about fishing anyway? But my hunch is that Jesus chose fishermen because fishermen hold a gritty kind of faith, full of persistence and positioning. It's not wishful thinking; it's participatory. Jesus doesn't want people throwing pennies into stagnant fountains. He wants people bravely throwing the lines of their lives into moving tides, trusting that he will be faithful through every ebb and every flow. Jesus showed Peter and the other men that when all looks dead and you've exhausted your strength, go ahead and let down your net one more time. He showed them that depending on him will always yield a greater catch than trying to live in your own strength.

Jeremiah 31:35 says, "This is what the Lord says, he who

* Matthew 13:47.

appoints the sun to shine by day, who decrees the moon and stars to shine by night, who stirs up the sea so that its waves roar—the LORD Almighty is his name."

In the falling-tide seasons of life, do we trust the God who stirs up the sea? Will we depend on the one who the winds and the waves obey? Is it possible that when all we see is change, transition, and churning, the waters are being stirred up optimally for our good?

Your soul needs an anchor, and even though it formerly felt tethered to your spouse, your job, your old home, your old community, or whatever changed in your life, God wants to use this transition as a place where you are propelled into his presence. He wants hope in him to be the anchor for your soul.* This season might already be marked by confusion or disillusionment, but don't let those be the only things it's marked by. It can be marked by God's presence too. You might look back on this season and never wish to go through it again—but you also might look back on it and say, "I know God deeply because of it."

If I want to think like a fisherman—like Grandpa Bob—I have to trust that underneath all the foaming and roaring and receding of the sea is potential. Potential is what the kingdom is all about: the tiny mustard seed with the potential to grow into a huge tree and the fishing net with the potential to pull in all kinds of fish.† There is potential in this season for you to grow beyond what you thought possible, learn lessons you will never forget, and catch something from God you wouldn't have caught in a dormant season. There is potential for you to encounter God in a new way, discover his strength in your weakness, and learn the power of daily dependence on him. There is potential to develop new rhythms and ways of

* Hebrews 6:19.

† Matthew 13:31–32, 47–52.

relating to God that will mark your life forever. There is potential for you to see the goodness of God on display while you learn how to let go of the tight grip of control over every outcome. If we want to embrace life with fisherman-like grit, we need to lean into that potential, not lean out.

We can choose to view falling tide like everyone else: a transition that just happens, a necessary ebb in life. Or we can view falling tide like a fisherman: the moment to wait for, prepare for, and anticipate. We might not know how long it will take, how big the catch will be, or how effortlessly we will carry the catch, but we can expect that God will be faithful as we learn to depend on him. We can trust the goodness of God without setting an expectation for exactly what his goodness will look like. He will demonstrate his love and faithfulness, and he will use it all to grow our souls, because life's deepest lessons don't come from dormant waters.

Pray It Through

God, thank you for the lessons you have waiting for me in this time of transition. Teach me what you want me to see and know in this season. Help me to reach for you, your Word, your people, and the right places. Help me to walk in wisdom and clarity and to hear your voice louder than ever before. Amen.

Anchor Your Soul

1. What were some of your unspoken expectations about your answer to prayer?
   - *I expected it to be easier.*
   - *I expected to feel different.*
   - *I expected to handle it more confidently.*
   - *I expected it to come without a major curveball.*
   - *I expected . . .*
2. What are some specific reward prediction errors you've experienced in this season?
3. In what ways are you learning to depend on God? Finish the prayers below:
   - *God, I am depending on you daily for . . .*
   - *God, I am learning to rely on your strength in moments when I feel . . .*
   - *God, thank you for teaching me . . .*
   - *God, I know I'm growing because you are showing me . . .*
4. What are some of the ways God has shown you his faithfulness in this season, even if it has looked different than you expected?

Chapter 3

GOOD GRIEF!

Feeling sad after making the right decision doesn't mean it was the wrong decision.

—DR. CAROLINE LEAF

You finally arrive at the moment you prayed for—baby in arms, contract signed, ribbon cut, vows spoken—only your heart feels . . . *off.* And because you didn't feel *what* you were supposed to feel, *when* you were supposed to feel it, it made you wonder if you made a big mistake. Shouldn't good feelings automatically follow good decisions and good changes? Shouldn't joy accompany all the positive milestones in our lives? The problem is this: Emotions are complicated, and they don't always stay in their lane.

Society isn't good at recognizing that it's normal to feel mixed emotions. We assume we are supposed to be either happy *or* sad, excited *or* depressed, rejoicing *or* grieving—but a cocktail of emotions? We don't know what to do with that. Welcome to the weird and wonderful world of what I like to call Good Grief.

Here are a few ways Good Grief shows up during seasons of change:

1. We experience a measure of sadness that doesn't seem to match the situation (like the Season of Balancing I talked about in a previous chapter) or is more intense than we expected.
2. We discover unexpected grief is surfacing from something that happened a long time ago but is demanding to be processed *now* (inconvenient timing, I know).
3. We are in a Bittersweet Season, holding a blessing in one hand and a curveball in the other (also not the greatest timing, but hardship doesn't check our calendars first).

If you've ever felt like your emotions are too much or if you were raised in a family that allowed only happy feelings at the dinner table, you're not alone. Maybe you were taught to stuff your emotions down, pray them away, or fake a smile. This chapter is a gentle nudge to say it's okay. Your unexpected grief doesn't disqualify your faith or negate your gratitude. You can still love Jesus and cry in the shower.

RAIN ON A SUNNY DAY

Growing up in Oregon, if the forecast said rain, I could pretty much count on a gray, soggy day from start to finish. But after I moved to Florida, I noticed something strange: The forecast for rain wasn't permanent, and a sunny day didn't come without random spurts of rain. Florida's unique atmosphere creates concentrated rain showers, meaning it can be pouring on one street and dry a few blocks over. And showers can pass through quickly; rain often comes in bursts—a sudden downpour, then sunshine again. (If it's raining, don't worry, you still might be able to hit the beach. Just give it another twenty minutes or so.) At first it felt wrong, like the sky mixed up its signals. But over time I realized this is just how it works. Sunshine and rain don't cancel each other out here; they coexist.

Some emotions are like the Florida weather; they show up suddenly, unexpectedly, and often in the middle of your sunny day. But the good news? The forecast for Good Grief is less like the Oregon rain that persists and more like the Florida rain that comes in bursts.

BRIANNE'S SEASON OF BALANCING

My friend Brianne knows a bit about emotions raining on her parade (well, on her newlywed season that is). She had been planning her winter-wonderland wedding ever since she was a little girl. Her December outdoor ceremony in Rhode Island amid trees flecked with snow couldn't have been more perfect, despite those who told her she was crazy. Nobody ended up frozen, and her guests still reminisce about the whimsy of it all years later. Yet the days and months following Brianne's wedding didn't match the honeymoon phase everyone hypes up. The wedding day went off without a hitch; she married the love of her life and couldn't have been happier as a newlywed. Still, she sank into an unexplainable feeling that went beyond postwedding blues and even googled "postwedding depression" to confirm she wasn't the only bride to feel this way. She tucked her wedding dress into a suitcase, never to be opened again. Even her wedding-video highlight reel sent tears rolling down her face. Years later, even though the unexpected grieving has passed, she still vividly remembers that time in her life—a time when sadness pounced at the most inopportune time. So much time, energy, and planning went into her dream wedding, and she never considered what it would feel like after it was all over.

It turns out Brianne is not alone. According to *Psychology Today*, over 50 percent of new brides report feelings of sadness or letdown after their weddings, and about 12 percent experience clinical-level depression within six months.[1] Newlyweds often feel depressed, because when the excitement and attention from wedding planning suddenly vanish, the reality of settling into a new routine feels anticlimactic.[2] *The Guardian* reported that postwedding anxiety is common too. Nightmares, guilt, and low-level anxiety—triggered by unmet expectations and the reality of everything having to be perfect—are normal.[3]

Research shows that after major highs in life (like weddings, graduations, or job changes), people often experience a natural emotional downturn. Psychologists call it the "comedown effect."[4] Neuroscience explains that once the anticipation ends, our brains recalibrate, which can feel like a letdown even when life is good.

I watched a documentary about an engaged couple who traveled around the world to experience the customs of weddings and marriages in other countries. In one Tujia village in China, the bride undergoes a weeklong weeping ritual with female family members and neighbors before the wedding. The ceremonial "crying marriage" is intended to help the bride mourn the end of her former life and bring emotional closure before the new stage.[5] Maybe they were onto something. Maybe we'd have less postwedding depression cases if we got all our tears out ahead of time. Who knows?

Brianne's experience reminds me of when runners cross the finish line of a marathon and tears accompany their triumph. It turns out, it's called runner's cry. The combination of physical exhaustion, hormone release, and the abrupt end of adrenaline and anticipation creates an emotional crash.[6] This reaction is not unlike the baby blues I experienced in the weeks after I gave birth to my son. This hormonal sadness affects 50 to 75 percent of new mothers and usually resolves within a couple of weeks (unlike postpartum depression, which is more intense and can last months or over a year).[7]

Sometimes we know a good life change will come with a little sadness, but we get blindsided by the timing or the intensity. I heard a woman on the radio describe her experience sending her son off to college. She and her son both agreed it would be fun for him to go to college in another state and explore someplace new. She loved helping him through applications, touring colleges together, praying with him about the right choice, and guiding him to make his final decision. When he walked across the stage at graduation, she didn't shed a tear; she cheered at the top of her lungs. It was all exciting. Then a month later, seemingly out of nowhere, it hit her. She said, "It was a random Tuesday at 3:37 p.m. when I was folding a fitted sheet. I mean, fitted sheets are horrible, but it was more than that. My son was leaving. This would be the last time my son would live at home." She cried and cried and joked that she was catatonic for days. The dad piped in and said, "And that marked the beginning of getting slapped in the face with reality for the next twelve months."

Maybe you identify with Brianne in a Season of Balancing where your feelings don't seem to match your reality and you're trying to understand the confusing rain that arrived on your sunny day. Or maybe you're more like the woman sending her son off to college; you expected a little sadness, but you didn't expect a downpour.

We often unconsciously assign *what* we are supposed to feel, *when* we are supposed to feel it, *how long* it's supposed to last, and *how intense* it's supposed to be. But that can feel like trying to predict the weather; we get it right sometimes, and sometimes we get stuck trying to find an umbrella at the beach. Emotions are not as easy to wrangle or predict as we'd like, but the good news is they don't last forever.

IT'S ONLY NINETY SECONDS

I once heard the renowned Dr. Henry Cloud speak about the three *P*'s of dangerous thinking, explaining how we should avoid thinking things are personal, pervasive, and permanent. He shared that when we think things are personal, we see every setback as proof that there is something wrong with us. When that thinking pattern sets in, our brains begin to shut down and go to the next *P*, pervasive. Now what we're facing isn't just personal; it's everywhere. Everything is bad, and our whole lives suck. Then the kiss of death sets in, and we start to think it's all permanent, the third *P*. We believe life will always be this way, and it's never going to change. When we put the three *P*'s together, there's our prison.[8] When I first heard about the three *P*'s, I didn't realize I had bought into a narrative that everything was permanent. I sank into a pit of thinking my situation would never change, my emotions would never rebalance, my disorientation would last forever. I failed to remember what my mentor always says: "Melissa, nothing is permanent except for Jesus."

During my whirlwind of change fatigue, I got invited to go on a trip to Alaska with my grandma (Gigi). As we approached Icy Strait, Gigi kept mentioning that she wanted to do one of the excursions—namely, the world's largest zip line. I thought she was kidding, so I played along. It wasn't until she was standing at the ticket counter buying tickets for both of us that I realized this wasn't a joke.

"I-I-I-I'm afraid of heights, Grandma. I can't go with you." I went on to add another handful of excuses to make my point. The lady at the counter said, "You can't let your grandma go by herself! Besides, are you really going to let *your grandma* be braver than you are?" Like a schoolyard bully, she taunted me. I stared back at her waiting for her to give me grace.

Before I knew it we were on a gondola headed to the top. As I looked at the trees below me, my mind scanned for ways to get out of doing the zip line. I'm a bookworm, not a thrill seeker. I asked the guide if it was possible to go back down once I was up there. He said, "No, ma'am. It's really not possible. It's a half-mile hike to get there, and if we send you back on your own, you'll get attacked by bears." Well—thanks, Alaska.

The zip line was taller than the Empire State Building. It travels sixty to seventy miles per hour and is 5,330 feet in length. It is the world's largest with a vertical drop of 1,300 feet. They try to sell you on the "sweeping views" of Port Frederick and Icy Strait, but who cares about the views when you're going to die, right?

I'm embarrassed to admit my grandma was the one trying to calm me down. She comforted me and told me it was okay if I wanted to back out. She danced a jig as we stood in line, reminding me this was going to be "soooo much fuuuuuun!" (And the world's coolest grandma award goes to Gigi!) Gigi told me it's ninety seconds from top to bottom. When I heard that, it was the first time I felt like I could do it.

It's only ninety seconds.

I can survive for ninety seconds.

I kept telling myself that number over and over again.

Ninety seconds.

Ninety seconds.

Ninety seconds.

Even though the skin on my face felt like it was going to fall off, I survived. I didn't enjoy one single second of the ninety, but hey, I lived to tell the story, right?

The only thing that gave this bookworm the courage to plunge 5,330 feet was knowing that it would last only a short time. Looking back, I know the fear was real but so was the truth that it would pass. And that's how grief can feel too. It may come out of nowhere, like a burst of rain on a sunny Florida afternoon or hit like a zip-line drop when you least expect it. But it doesn't last forever. Sometimes all we need is the reminder that we can hold on for a little longer. The wave passes, the tears dry up, and the storm runs out of rain. We need this reminder, because sometimes fear hits midblessing, grief shows up on our happiest day, and the clouds roll in when we were expecting sunshine. It doesn't mean we're broken; it means we're human. We're here for this ride called life, and the Good Grief (and not-so-good grief) that comes along with it.

And as it turns out, if you hold on through the drop, the sun breaks through again—and your face doesn't fall off.

THE UNANNOUNCED HOUSEGUEST

My friend Jenee moved to Florida shortly after we did. Her husband got an amazing promotion, they bought a beautiful new home, and the kids were doing great. Everything on the outside was an answer to her prayers. Yet she began having panic attacks accompanied by unexpected bouts of crying. If everything was good and she was living in an answer to prayer, why did she feel depressed? Jenee visited a therapist who helped her realize that she hadn't processed the emotions of her mom's passing two years prior. Life had been a whirlwind of pregnancies (triplets and twins!), and she hadn't stopped to take a breath and fully grieve the death of her mom. Jenee and I sat over coffee with our minds blown: "Grief can creep up on you? Something you went through years ago can pop up in your life and demand to be processed?"

What most people don't realize is that even good change can bring to the surface hurt or trauma they tried to bury when they didn't know how to cope with it.

I heard a line from the movie *The Gorge* that stuck with me: "You bury enough secrets, the graveyard runs out of room."[9] Although I haven't buried secrets in my life, I've been a professional gravedigger when it comes to burying trauma. Shortly after I gave my life to Jesus in college, I heard a pastor end his sermon with, "You don't need to go to therapy. All you need is a touch from Jesus." So I responded to the altar call that day, received prayer, and buried anything that tried to surface thereafter. God can do anything, but he did not heal all my childhood trauma in an instant that day, and clearly my graveyard ran out of room. (It turns out Jesus uses therapists too.)

Jenee and I were both in similar Bittersweet Seasons, enjoying God's blessings but also experiencing unexpected grief. Grief is hard enough on its own, but when it ambushes you, it's disorienting. I expected grief to be linear, but it turns out it's more like the houseguest who drops by unannounced.

Maybe there's something in your life that happened months or years ago, and the grief is knocking at your door now. You're trying to have a party, and he's the guest you didn't invite for a reason. Yet the unexpected houseguest demands to be let in. Maybe you're afraid to open the door, so you keep holding back your tears and stuffing down your feelings.

If this sounds like you, I've got good news and bad news. The bad news is that you need to let the houseguest in or he will keep knocking. Trying to resist negative emotions only makes things worse in the long run, because what you resist persists. Brené Brown once explained that "you cannot selectively numb emotions."[10] You cannot choose which ones you want to feel and which ones you'd rather dismiss. In trying to numb negative emotions, you numb positive ones, too, and end up feeling them less. So go ahead, unlock the door.

Here's the good news: A houseguest is a visitor, not a permanent family member. Some people avoid beginning the grieving process because they're afraid of opening a valve that won't ever shut. Although it's true some grief never fully goes away (like the death of a loved one), it doesn't mean we live a life of perpetual waterworks.

In the Beatitudes Jesus said, "Blessed are those who mourn."* It can also be translated as "Blessed are those who grieve" or "Blessed are those who weep." Not exactly the kind of beatitude we stitch on throw pillows. The Greek word used in the New Testament is

* Matthew 5:4.

pentheó, signifying intimate, intense, heart-breaking sorrow. Jesus didn't say, "Blessed are the joyful, the strong, the ones who've got it all together." Nope, he started with grief. (Good Grief, right?)

Recently, I shared a small piece of advice with a grieving friend. I couldn't answer all the whys for her situation or even my own. But what I could offer was a simple truth: Even though some grief doesn't go away fully, living in constant survival mode does. At first you're in survival mode every day, wondering if you'll ever feel like yourself again. It's scary, and it feels like it's going to last forever; you worry it's going to become your new norm. And then, one week you realize you were in survival mode for only six days. You got one good day—one little glimmer of normalcy. Eventually the six days a week become five and then four. Grief will always find a way to pop by unannounced, but in the bigger picture it's comforting to know that daily survival mode does not last forever as you learn to find ways to cope, grieve, and adjust to your new norm.

When my kids were little, I used to say to myself, *This won't last forever.* I said it with a nostalgic feeling, a reminder that it's special, and I wanted to soak up every moment. Ironically, in difficult seasons I find myself saying the same thing, *This won't last forever.* I say it as encouragement that the hardship will get easier and the difficult season will pass. So whether you are in an "Aw, this won't last forever" or an "Ugh [deep breath], this won't last forever" season, change is inevitable. And depending on where you are right now, that can bring a sense of sadness or a sense of relief.

It might feel like the houseguest of grief has overstayed his welcome lately, but trust me when I say that he won't be staring you down when you're trying to sleep, stinking up your bathroom, or interrupting dinnertime forever. He will move on, and like the rain you wish would go away, he will come again another day.

HANNAH'S BITTERSWEET SEASON

Grow, baby, grow!

That was my friend Hannah's constant prayer for her firstborn son while he was in the womb. Hannah and her husband would rub their hands over her belly and pray for their son's strength, health, and future. She prayed fervently for a healthy baby and smooth pregnancy, and she got what she prayed for. She had no complications during pregnancy, not even the typical nausea that most women get. It was a special season being pregnant for the first time, and Hannah soaked up every moment.

Even though Hannah dreamed of having a natural birth, her midwife suggested a thirty-nine-week induction. Her *Grow, baby, grow!* prayer worked a little too well. The little boy was not so little, and it was time for him to come out. Even though an induction wasn't what Hannah planned, after praying, she agreed and trusted in God's timing.

Hannah's labor didn't go exactly as hoped. Despite hours of intense contractions and increasing medication, Hannah's body wasn't progressing. After eight hours and little dilation, it was clear that the baby was stuck and a C-section was necessary. Though it was the last thing Hannah wanted, she felt an inexplicable calm as she entered the operating room, and her son Callen was born at 6:25 p.m.—healthy, big, and beautiful. The miracle of life was right in front of their eyes, and their hearts were bursting with joy. But after the delivery Hannah noticed the medical team becoming tense. Her doctor said to her, "We don't know exactly what's happening, but you are bleeding uncontrollably. We are doing everything possible to avoid a hysterectomy." The doctors tried everything: manual compression, medications, but nothing worked. They had to put

Hannah under anesthesia. She didn't fully understand what was going on or how severe it was; she was even cracking jokes before they put her under. Little did she know that for nearly an hour, doctors were fighting to save her life and her uterus. Ultimately, they could save only one. When she woke up around nine p.m., her uterus was gone.

The first few hours after surgery were a blur. Hannah was mentally aware but emotionally detached. Since she was still medicated and foggy in the brain, the weight of what happened hadn't sunk in. For the next two days, doctors monitored her hour by hour to ensure her organs didn't shut down. Her husband fielded calls to family, while hoping he wouldn't lose the love of his life and become a single dad on the same day.

On the third day a new nurse unknowingly touched the wound no one could see. As she examined Hannah's abdomen, she said, "Your uterus feels like it's in the right spot."

The mood in the room shifted.

The nurse said, "Are you okay? I feel like I said something wrong."

When Hannah explained she didn't have a uterus anymore, the nurse crumbled in tears on the floor. Hannah's heart crumbled too. It was the first moment the fog lifted and it became real: The pregnancy she savored with Callen would be her last. She would never be able to give birth to another child.

For months Hannah tried to bypass the pain. But grief didn't ask permission or wait for Callen to grow up; it just knocked on Hannah's door and continued to knock. She never expected an ad for tampons to cause her so much pain. And every time she received a "Congratulations," it was met with a sting of mixed emotions. *They don't know the whole story.* When a government foundation made a routine call to ask Hannah what birth control she was going to use to make sure she didn't get pregnant again so soon, she began to spiral.

As a strong believer in Jesus, she knew God could use her circumstances, but she didn't want him to, because she didn't want this to be her story. It was hard to accept. There were sweet moments with Callen that she was immensely grateful for: his first smiles, sleepy snuggles, the newborn smell that enveloped her heart. Hannah was full of love but also full of a quiet ache that whispered, *This is the last time.*

Hannah's healing journey started when she decided to share her story on social media. She wanted to feel fully known (since she felt like she was lying every time she posted a happy picture of Callen). Eventually she also reached out to a therapist. She wrote letters, she cried, and she began to process her traumatic birth experience and the reality it left her with. She had to learn to walk through the journey of holding gratitude for Callen in one hand and grief in the other.

In time Hannah realized it didn't have to be the end of her story. When she told her counselor about her idea to adopt, her counselor wanted to make sure she wasn't trying to trade one hard thing for another. Hannah knew that, in a way, she was, but adoption had also been on her heart long before she brought it up to her counselor. It was something she'd been quietly researching and pouring herself into. Could it be that something hard was pushing her toward one of her holy longings? It was Callen's first birthday when Hannah and her husband made the decision to adopt. They started the home-study process the following week. The adoption agency said, "This will go as fast as you can complete the paperwork, likely two months." But Hannah, with her heart eager and ready, finished the paperwork in three weeks. (She was already well researched.) Hannah and her husband were matched with their son

Tatum, who was born about nine months after they started the process. Tatum may not have grown in Hannah's belly, but she grew him in her heart. They have now adopted two boys: Tatum, then Wade. Hannah's Bittersweet Season was not the end of her story. It was a comma, not a period. And through it all she learned that God can answer the prayer to *Grow, baby, grow!* in more ways than one.

It's a confusing road when it's paved with both joy and heartache. For anyone like Hannah who had to carry something happy and heavy at the same time, it can feel like getting emotional whiplash. That's when you learn to walk through the Valley of Baka, a place where sorrow and sacredness somehow meet: "Blessed are those whose strength is in you, whose hearts are set on pilgrimage. As they pass through the Valley of Baka, they make it a place of springs; the autumn rains also cover it with pools. They go from strength to strength, till each appears before God in Zion."*

In this beautiful psalm the author used the pilgrimage through the Valley of Baka to illustrate a difficult path. The valley's name indicates a dry and parched region where weeping trees grow. It was known as the Valley of Tears. As people traveled to Jerusalem to worship, they would pass through this "weeping" place, but their journey proved to be worth it in the end. Their Valley of Baka turned into refreshing springs and pools, and they increased in strength until they appeared before God. The location of the Valley of Baka is unknown, and it's mentioned only in this verse, which leads scholars to believe that the psalmist's intention was to share a figurative principle: Those who follow God can expect to pass through hard valleys, valleys that God will be with them in. Weeping places aren't dwelling places; they are byways to God's

* Psalm 84:5–7.

presence. It's a weeping place but also a place of strengthening. It's a place of tears but also a place of trust.

The first part of this Valley of Baka passage is a reminder that we are blessed to find our strength in him—the unchanging one, the constant one, the one who is with us before, during, and after our pilgrimage. Whether you're in a Season of Building, a Bittersweet Season, or a Season of Balancing, God's fixed nature ensures that his love will be with you no matter what.

The second part of the passage holds an equally important lesson: The weeping place is not permanent, and the pilgrimage leads to redemption and strength. When you're in a weeping place, it feels like your time there is never going to end. It feels like you're going to wake up every morning wiping away tears. Sometimes the most comforting reminder is that every step forward is a step toward strength. Every new day is one day closer to feeling like yourself again. Every step toward honesty and healing is a step toward trusting your Creator with the rest of your story—Good Grief and all.

Pray It Through

God, I give you any grief and mismatched or mixed emotions I'm experiencing. I thank you that my feelings aren't final. I pray that you would help me process anything that's unresolved and give me strength when I'm weary or overwhelmed. I invite your peace, clarity, and assurance for the future. Thank you for your steady hand in my life. Help me walk with you all the days of my life. Amen.

Anchor Your Soul

STEP 1: NAME WHAT YOU MISS

Write down what (or who) you're grieving. Be specific.

- I miss . . .
- I wish . . .
- I never got to . . .

STEP 2: RELEASE THE "SHOULDS"

Write down the lies that circulate feelings such as guilt or shame or the pressure you've carried in grief—the statements that begin with "I should" or "I shouldn't still." Here are a few examples:

- I should be over this by now.
- I shouldn't cry when I talk about it.
- I should have handled it differently.

Then draw a line through them. Now write out truths, such as

- I'm human, and mixed emotions are allowed.
- God invites me to come as I am.
- It's okay to process, grieve, and still need time.

STEP 3: REMEMBER GOD'S NEARNESS

Finish this sentence (as a prayer):

God, I need you to meet me in my grief by . . .

Then reflect on this Scripture:

The Lord is close to the brokenhearted
*and saves those who are crushed in spirit.**

Take a few deep breaths and imagine God's presence with you—not fixing, not rushing, just with you, inviting you to come as you are.

* Psalm 34:18.

Chapter 4

GRATITUDE, GLIMMERS, GEMS, AND GUARDRAILS

The capacity for delight is the gift of paying attention.

—JULIA CAMERON

When was the last time you were *overwhelmed* with gratitude? Be honest. Not a word you wrote in your gratitude journal or a quick prayer before dinner. The kind of gratitude that nearly stops your heart. How long has it been? A week? Three months? Three years? Here's what I've discovered: If grief can stop by unannounced, so can gratitude. But if we want gratitude to visit more often, we need to learn how to roll out the red carpet for it.

At the beginning of this book, I told you that I believed you're grateful. Admitting that you're having difficulty adjusting to your new season doesn't preclude you from gratitude. I started calling my season "brutaful," because it was both brutal and beautiful. Giving my season this name was a way of reminding myself that both truths can exist; one doesn't cancel out the other. I held gratitude in one hand and grief in the other. But if I'm honest, gratitude felt limited, buried amid everything else going on. So why wasn't gratitude popping by more often during my season of change fatigue? I had so much to be grateful for, so why did gratitude feel stifled?

There's a lot of talk about triggers these days. We all have things that dysregulate us, remind us of the past, or make us feel a wave of sadness or grief. But have you heard of the opposite of a trigger? A glimmer. That's probably not the technical name for it, but it's a term used to describe being overwhelmed by gratitude.

Here's an example of a glimmer: When my kids were little, they would fall asleep on my chest. The chubby cheeks, the baby smell, and the tender moment of knowing there was no place else we'd rather be—it was overwhelming indeed. My heart felt like it would burst out of my chest and explode into a million pieces. Tears welled up in my eyes, and for a moment it felt like heaven kissed earth right there on my chest. Glimmers came every day; sometimes multiple times a day.

Around the time my whole world changed, my kids were all growing up. No more babies or toddlers falling asleep on my chest. No more piggyback rides. No more sticky fingers reaching out to hold my hand. It all happened without warning. Suddenly I wasn't Mommy anymore. I was Mom—or sometimes bruh. I was no longer invited to playdates, and all the toys were boxed up, ready to be donated. I call this chapter of my life my mom-life crisis, because it felt like I was losing a part of myself. I didn't expect to be closing a chapter of motherhood while I was growing my family through adoption. And I know every child grows up—I should have seen it coming. Yet it still hit me like a freight train.

So what do you do when all the things that used to give you glimmers are gone, and now it feels like all you're left with are your triggers? I sat and talked over coffee with one mom who was an empty nester. She said, "I loved raising my kid so much that sometimes I wonder if there will ever be anything in my life that compares to motherhood." She spoke out loud what I was wondering.

Are my glimmers gone?

Will I ever feel overwhelmed with gratitude the way I did back then?

Were glimmers just a chapter—a closed chapter—that I'll never get back?

Are my best days behind me?

Or is it possible to cultivate and grow glimmers and overwhelming gratitude in our lives, even if we are closing a chapter we loved? Is it possible to lean in and enjoy our answers to prayer, to squeeze every glimmer out of it? Is it possible to look back on this season of our lives and know (even amid complicated feelings) that we enjoyed it to the fullest? I think so, but we've got some work to do.

HOLY PAUSES

Here's one undeniable truth: Life with five kids is busier than life with three. Going back to work full-time and adding a daily commute, kids' activities, and therapy made it that much busier. Here's another undeniable truth: The busier you are, the harder it is to appreciate your life. John Mark Comer said, "[Hurry] kills joy, gratitude, appreciation; people in a rush don't have time to enter the goodness of the moment."[1]

While the tender years of raising littles is a precious season indeed, nap times wrapped holy pauses into my day that I never considered holy at the time. They were moments when my biggest priority was to be still, literally. *Don't. Wake. The. Sleeping. Baby.*

Psalm 46:10 says, "Be still, and know that I am God." Stillness allows us to notice the blessings and goodness of God right in front of us. Stillness gives us the mental margin to remember that we are living in an answer to prayer. Stillness reminds us that this is not a season to sprint through; it is a season to savor. So, what if the reason I wasn't experiencing as many glimmers (and only noticing the triggers) was because I lost the rhythm of holy pauses?

I recently took a trip to London, and I heard one local say, "Every day I rush to work and see crowds of tourists taking pictures. Most of the time the crowds annoy me, because I'm in a hurry to get to work. But every once in a while, I stop and notice what they're looking at. I look up at a cathedral or the Tower of London and think to myself, *Wow. That really is beautiful, isn't it?*"

For those of us who are believers in Jesus, I think we should be the best at noticing God's creation and gifts all around us. We should be professional noticers. Other people might pass by beauty without noticing, without appreciating, or without thanking, but we should be people who know how to be still and notice. We should be people who stir up gratitude even on days when it feels like it's playing hide-and-seek. We should make it our aim not to rush but to be noticers. Jennifer Dukes Lee said, "We need permission to take our time, to marvel, to wonder and ponder and savor, and to move at the un-hurried pace of Christ. Time is not a commodity to be used but a gem to be treasured."[2]

When I think of a glimmer, I am reminded of an ember. It's a tiny glowing spark that holds the potential for the warmth of a fire. It's the smallest flicker of light in our day that, if fanned into flame, can birth a life full of overflowing gratitude. But when we have too many logs packed tightly in a fire, they don't leave enough oxygen to keep the flame alive. When we have too many logs on the fire in our lives, we don't have the space to notice, to take holy pauses, or to fan the embers of gratitude. It's possible to become so consumed with managing the gift that we no longer acknowledge the Giver. And in doing so, we are robbed of fully appreciating the gift. We've got all the logs but no fire.

A glimmer for me is much more than an emotional experience. It's when God's presence meets my soul's deepest expression of gratitude. It's as if the Holy Spirit climbs inside these moments and says, *Yes, child, here I am. I've been waiting for you to notice.* It's when I'm so preoccupied, busy, and anxious that I lose touch with the frequency of gratitude. I have to slow down. I have to take a holy pause.

Around AD 525 a man named Benedict structured eight daily prayers for monks. He set rules so that he could help each monk live as close to the life shown in the gospels as possible. When the monks heard a signal, they would stop work immediately to be with God. The idea was that creating a continual ritual would help them more easily access the presence of God throughout the day. They were taking holy pauses to remember the purpose behind their work. These moments are a reminder of a truth that "in him we live and move and have our being."*

What signals do you have in your day that remind you to

---

* Acts 17:28.

take a holy pause? What reminds you to slow down and savor the moment? Sometimes a holy pause can be spontaneous, but what if Benedict was onto something? What if the holy pauses we structure into our day (whether it's a calendar reminder or a morning walk) are the keys to ensuring we welcome more gratitude into our lives?

Some cultures value pauses in their day so much, they have terms for their pauses:

- *La dolce far niente* (Italy). Translated as "the sweetness of doing nothing," the joy of leisurely, unstructured time and appreciating the moment without feeling guilty.
- *Sobremesa* (Spain). The leisurely time spent at the table after a meal, enjoying conversation and company without rushing.
- *Flâner* (France). The art of strolling aimlessly, particularly in cities, simply to take in the atmosphere.
- *Hygge* (Denmark). A sense of coziness and contentment, often associated with simple pleasures, warmth, and relaxation.
- *Fika* (Sweden). A coffee break (which usually involves a sweet pastry) that is about deliberately slowing down and connecting with friends and family.
- *Niksen* (the Netherlands). A word that literally means "doing nothing." It encourages idleness and allows the mind to wander as a form of rest.

My holy pauses may look different now than when my babies fell asleep on my chest. But I'm determined that glimmers will not be a thing of the past. Recently I was watching my newest daughter at her swimming lesson. I felt an invitation to notice—a nudge from the Holy Spirit. I set my phone down and immersed myself in the moment. I remembered how she used to be afraid of jumping in the pool, how she trembled on the edge in a panic. And now here she was, jumping in with a smile on her face, waving at me after she mastered her new swim stroke.

For a moment my mind panned out to remember how far we've come. I remembered how I was once a traumatized girl who needed a family, and now here she was, a traumatized girl who needed a family. My life came full circle in a flash. I may never have a memory of holding her on my chest as a baby, but I have moments like this where I stand up and cheer for her swimming victories and her whole precious existence. And suddenly my heart bursts out of my chest and explodes into a million pieces, just like it did back then. Tears form in the corners of my eyes. Heaven kisses earth, even in the teenage years. *That's my girl.*

Notice. Holy pause. Glimmer.

USE NOSTALGIA AS A BRIDGE, NOT A BARRIER

Often we see the past through rose-colored lenses. I remember my kids' baby smell, the chubby cheeks, and the glimmers that came with them. But to be honest, I seldom think about the sleepless nights or the temper tantrums. I want a rewind button, but being around moms with babies or toddlers for an afternoon reminds me of how exhausting those years were. Nostalgia isn't a bad thing unless the joy of the past robs you of the joy of the present.

In the book of Exodus, the Israelites were stuck wandering in the wilderness for forty years. They weren't slaves anymore. They didn't have forced labor all day long. They were no long less than; they were equals. They had a purpose (getting to the promised land) to look forward to. But the problem was, everything was different. The food was different. Their daily routine was different. Their surroundings were different. Even the culture was different. So, after hundreds of years of slavery, the Israelites were free and thrust into a change they had prayed for. But instead of expressing gratitude, they grumbled and complained, and at one point they thought it would be better to go back to Egypt.* Even though it's what they had prayed for, different is still hard. The Israelites were in a Season of Balancing. They were experiencing mismatched emotions and needed to learn how to guard against unhealthy nostalgia. Here's what A. J. Swoboda said in his book *The Dusty Ones*: "In responding to their liberation by complaining, Israel commits the sin of nostalgia—living in the past and failing to recognize the holiness of the present. Nostalgia is seeing God as the Alpha of our beginning, the Omega of our end, but not as the God of every letter in between. Nostalgia refuses to see God in the now."[3]

We will all be taken back by pictures, memories, places, songs, and even smells. But how do we avoid falling into a pit of unhealthy nostalgia so that we can see God in the now? First, we need to let nostalgia be a bridge, not a barrier. If songs, places, and even smells can take us back, we need a practice that reminds us of what God is doing right now. I begin with a short prayer. When nostalgia brings the rose-colored lenses, I pray, *Thank you, God, for what you did then, but I also thank you for what you are doing now.* I'll get specific about the things I appreciate about that memory or that season of my life and thank him for strengthening me through

---

* Exodus 16:2–4.

the hard times during that time period, then I'll get specific about the ways God is showing up in my life in the current season, and I'll end by thanking him for his faithfulness through *every* season. With this small practice, nostalgia becomes a bridge to gratitude, not a barrier to it. It also helps to recall the toughest part of that past season, which takes away the illusion that rose-colored lenses bring. I'll show you exactly how to do this for yourself at the end of this chapter.

YOU FIND WHAT YOU'RE LOOKING FOR

I once tried my luck at a treasure-hunt game. The goal was to dig through a treasure chest filled with sand to find the white gems. The tricky part was that the chest was full of other colored gems (of the same size), but only the white ones counted toward the prize. Even though the gems felt the same, I had to examine each one to see if it was the right color. There were seven total white gems, and I had thirty seconds to find as many as possible. I swept through the sand with my fingers, pulling up gems every other second. Blue. Green. Purple. Yellow. None of them were white. (I had heard whispers that the white gems were hard to find, so I felt better. It wasn't just me; it was a hard game.)

The girl who went after me missed her calling as a treasure hunter, for sure. I don't know how she did it. In hyperspeed, she dug through the sand with her hands, and every gem she pulled out was white. One after another, until all seven white gems sat in her hand in under thirty seconds. The host of the game looked bewildered. "No one's ever found this many white gems before." He was so shocked, I think he forgot he was supposed to give out a prize. Here's my point to this treasure-hunt story: Gratitude is as effortless for some people as scooping up seven white gems was for the girl in the treasure hunt. Some people see a heap of sand and quickly find every gem inside. It's a superpower. And then there are those like me who can't find even one.

Gratitude comes more easily to some people than others. Like driving a car when the alignment is off, some people's focus always veers toward the ditch. Call it brain chemistry, personality, or even culture, but some people's minds automatically find what's wrong with a picture before they ever consider what's right. They can walk into a beautiful room but hyperfixate on a small stain on the carpet. They can see a stunning photo but immediately spot the imperfection. Their attention to detail can be a gift that drives everyone to excellence (and can also drive them crazy). Those people have to work harder, dig deeper and longer, to find gratitude, but it doesn't make the gratitude any less genuine. The same amount of white gems were in that other girl's treasure chest as in mine; she was just quicker at finding them. What took her thirty seconds would have taken me an hour, but eventually we would have held the same number of white gems.

My mentor, Julie Gorman, always says, "You find what you're looking for." If you look for reasons to be hopeless, you'll find them. If you look for reasons to be grateful, you'll find those too. Some of us need to look a little longer and harder for those gems—those glimpses of what God is doing in our lives right now. Especially in seasons when we are overwhelmed with change fatigue, we need to play a game of I spy and diligently look for evidence of God's faithfulness. We will find what we're looking for, so let's stop veering toward the ditch and start looking for gems. It might require more digging, but gratitude has the power to change your life.

In case you don't believe me, research shows that regularly

practicing gratitude leads to greater happiness, reduced stress, and improved mental and physical health. Grateful individuals sleep better, tend to act more selflessly, and have a more optimistic mindset.[4] Gratitude exercises, like journaling or prayers of thanksgiving, have lasting effects in boosting happiness and lowering depressive symptoms. So expressing gratitude is not a waste of time or just feeling positive vibes. It's inviting God's presence and power into your life. And if you need that in scientific terms, it's literally improving your health and happiness.

Part of navigating my mom-life crisis was learning how to shift my focus from grief to gratitude. I was grieving closing a chapter of littles much more than I expected. To make matters worse, I watched other moms seem to handle this transition without flinching, "But it's great! Teenagers are so fun!" They didn't acknowledge an ounce of grief, which made me feel worse. "Yeah, it's totally great!" I'd say in agreement, wondering if I was the only mom who was having a hard time coping with the transition. It's true—teenagers are great, and I love my kids at every stage. But did anyone else feel an ache in their hearts over the plastic horsies that no longer lined the bathtub or the jammies that no longer fit? *Just me? Great.*

One text message changed everything. I still reread it when I'm having a hard time shifting my grief to gratitude. My friend sent this: "The baby girl I was telling you about . . . she passed away yesterday morning. They didn't give details, just complications from surgery."

The day I got that text, I gasped and fell to my knees in prayer for the family. It was a wake-up call. Yes, my children are growing much faster than I'd prefer. But they are growing. They are alive, and they are growing. This is what I cling to when time feels unfair and my child's hand feels like it's doubled in size in a year. It's growing. And even though it feels like the worst thing, it's really the best thing.

It's hard to make the switch from growing your family to watching them grow, but some parents are mourning a child they never got to watch grow. Change is hard; it feels unbearable at times. But painful growth is better than not getting the chance to grow at all. And when I read that text over again, my heart immediately shifts to gratitude.

God, thank you that my children are alive and growing.

Thank you that I get a front-row seat to every milestone in their lives.

Thanks for the gift of life. Thank you for another precious day with the people I love most.

That heartbreaking text message became a gem in my life—a reminder of how fragile and fleeting life is and a reminder to live every day with the kind of gratitude that baby's parents would have if they got one more day with their child. If I want to find reasons to grieve, I can find plenty. But when I'm ready to pull my head up and find gratitude, all I need to do is reach for that text message.

God will bring you gems like this—reminders that you can dig back up when gratitude feels buried. I have a note in my phone that reminds me of all the things I love about my husband (you understand, married people; sometimes you have to remind yourself of what you take for granted). I have notes in my phone that remind me of Scriptures, truths, and promises from God—notes I wrote when I was at my best to read when I'm at my worst.

You will find what you're looking for, so make sure you remember where you buried your gems. On your worst days—the days you feel like throwing yourself a pity party—your natural tendency is going to want to look for more reasons to sulk. If that's what you're looking for, you will find them.

Your coffee is cold.

Your teenager is in a mood.

The laundry is piling up.

The gas tank is empty.

But what if grumbling becomes an invitation to gratitude—a reminder to flip the script?

Your coffee is cold. *Thank you, God, that I get to start my day with coffee.*

Your teenager is in a mood. *Thank you that my teenager is healthy and growing.*

The laundry is piling up. *Thank you for all these clothes I have.*

The gas tank is empty. *Thank you that I own a car.*

If your mind naturally gravitates toward what's wrong, flip it and thank God for what's right. What are you taking for granted about the very thing you're grumbling about?

Maybe you're looking for reasons to be grateful and still having a hard time flipping the script. Instead of looking around, look up. Look to God's character: his faithfulness through every season, his unchanging nature, his steady hand, how he is a strong tower and a firm foundation. When our soul is parched, gratitude for the laundry might not go very far. We need to look to the essence of God. God's invitation is this: "You will seek me and find me when you seek me with all your heart."*

GUARDRAILS

A few years back I did something simple that changed my life. I turned off all the notifications on my phone and put it on

* Jeremiah 29:13.

silent—permanently. I decided I want to own my phone; I don't want my phone to own me. My husband and children are still puzzled.

"How do you know if you got a text?"

"How do you know if someone is calling you?"

Well, I check it when I feel like checking it. Sometimes I hear it vibrate, but mostly I pick up my phone when I want to. Why? Because my phone distracts me from the things that matter most. It's hard to cultivate gratitude, feel God's presence, or find glimmers in your life when you're constantly bombarded by the latest headline, group-text blast, insignificant email, or social media notification. (Maybe you're wondering how your child would get ahold of you in case of an emergency—there are settings for that.)

If you've lost traction in your relationship with God or your ability to worship, could it be that it's because of *dis*-traction? Traction is what keeps us on course and moving in the right direction. Yet too many of us live with too much distraction, and our attention is diverted to what's less important. When we get sidetracked, the distractions in life rob us of gaining traction, and we forget how to stop, notice, take a holy pause, and experience overwhelming gratitude.

John Ortberg said, "For many of us the great danger is not that we will renounce our faith. It is that we will become so distracted and rushed and preoccupied that we will settle for a mediocre version of it. We will just skim our lives instead of actually living them."[5]

It can be hard to find soul-gripping gratitude in a world full of distractions and discontentment. We often allow a thousand things to pull us away before we finally remember that it was God we were searching for all along. And there he was, right there amid our everyday, seemingly mundane lives.

It reminds me of the story of Ali Hafed. Ali was a wealthy Persian farmer, content with his life on his land of sprawling orchards, fields, and gardens. One day he was visited by a man who told him about the wealth hidden in diamonds. The man said, "Ali, if you can find a diamond mine, you'll become one of the richest men in the world."

That night Ali's contentment vanished, and the thought of diamonds consumed him. He decided to sell his farm and set off on a journey in search of diamonds, traveling across Persia, Palestine, and Europe—only to find nothing. Eventually, broke and hopeless, he threw himself into the sea and died.

Meanwhile, the man who bought Ali Hafed's farm was tending the land when he noticed a strange shiny black stone in a stream on the property. The stone turned out to be a diamond. The land Ali sold in his restlessness sat on what would become one of the richest diamond mines in history, the Golconda diamond mine in India.[6]

Ali got distracted by the idea of another life. Surely the grass was greener somewhere else. He was already rich (richer than he knew). He was already blessed. Gems were right under his feet. But instead of digging right where he was, he looked elsewhere. And so it is with gratitude.

What is it that's distracting you from the soil of gratitude you're standing on right now? Are the ads on television making you feel like you need another product to be happier? Are the curated images on social media robbing you of your contentment?

Is your phone being used as a tool for connection or a catalyst for comparison?

Is busyness and rushing leaving no room to stop and notice the gifts around you?

What *dis*traction made you lose your traction?

There are gems right under your feet. Dig for them. Notice them. Savor them. Protect them. Gratitude requires guardrails.

Pray It Through

God, help me grow in gratitude and glimmers in this season. Reveal to me the guardrails I need to put in place to protect and sustain a grateful heart, and help me to find the gems all around me. Thank you for your unwavering faithfulness through every season. Amen.

Anchor Your Soul

If you catch yourself falling into unhealthy nostalgia, you can follow my prayer structure for using nostalgia as a bridge and not a barrier. Here's what a prayer looks like that includes gratitude for the past, gratitude for hard times in that same season, gratitude for the present, and gratitude for God's unchanging character.

GRATITUDE FOR THE PAST

God, thank you for all those moments when my babies fell asleep on my chest. I cherish those memories.

GRATITUDE FOR THE HARD TIMES IN THAT SAME SEASON

I also thank you that you got me through all those sleepless nights and those difficult days of loneliness and for the way you carried me through the baby blues.

GRATITUDE FOR THE PRESENT

And I thank you for what you are doing right now. Thank you for the gift of teenagers. What a privilege it is to watch them grow. Thank you that I'm not lonely anymore and that you've brought me such great friends.

GRATITUDE FOR GOD'S UNCHANGING CHARACTER

Thank you that you were faithful then and you are still faithful now, and thank you that you hold beauty in every season. Amen.

Now, using the same format, form your own prayer.

GRATITUDE FOR THE PAST

God, thank you for . . .

GRATITUDE FOR THE HARD TIMES IN THAT SAME SEASON

I also thank you that you got me through . . .

GRATITUDE FOR THE PRESENT

And I thank you for what you are doing right now . . .

GRATITUDE FOR GOD'S UNCHANGING CHARACTER

Thank you that you were and are . . .

Amen.

Chapter 5

YOU'RE NOT STUCK; YOU'RE STRONG

Courage doesn't always roar. Sometimes courage is the quiet voice at the end of the day saying, "I will try again tomorrow."

—MARY ANNE RADMACHER

I know, you aren't supposed to feel stuck when you get your prayer answered, right? *Stuck* is only for those going through a crisis—the ones stuck with a difficult diagnosis, stuck in an abusive marriage, or stuck grieving the loss of a loved one. If you're anything like me, I had difficulty admitting I felt stuck. *How dare I?* But feeling stuck isn't reserved only for trials and tribulations. The truth is, we feel stuck when we feel stuck, and sometimes we don't need to have a big enough reason. We just are. And the sooner we can admit it, the sooner we can process it and move forward. Do you know who never gets unstuck? Someone who doesn't acknowledge they feel stuck. So I want to gently give you permission to admit that at least at times you feel stuck.

Maybe you're grateful for your new baby, but now you feel stuck at home on their sleep schedule. Or maybe you're grateful for your new business, but you feel stuck in exhaustion trying to sustain or grow it. You're grateful for your new job, but you feel stuck with a boss you don't align with or in a location that doesn't feel like home. Or maybe your answer to prayer is a dream come true, and you can't explain why you feel emotionally stuck; you just do. Being a human is complicated sometimes, isn't it?

Here's the good news when you feel stuck: God gets the opportunity to be the hero in your story. It's when we come to the end of ourselves that we depend on God the most. Maybe you've heard it all before. Maybe this sounds like a platitude we throw around to make ourselves feel better. But for those of us who have met God tangibly during times we felt most stuck, it's a truth we can't stop telling.

This chapter is for those of us in the messy middle. I'm going to show you how to reframe your stuck season so you can see that you are stronger than you think. Because sometimes strength is simply showing up anyway. Sometimes it's taking a deep breath and remembering your why on the days you want to quit. And sometimes it's taking a step back to remember that nothing you build with your hands will ever be big enough to satisfy your soul—only God can fill that gap.

WHY DON'T YOU GIVE UP?

"Why don't you just give up? God will forgive you," one person advised.

"Wh-wha-what?" I stammered, shocked at her suggestion. "I don't want to give up!"

"But you know you have the choice. You can give up if you want to," she added.

We sat in an awkward silence.

I wasn't expecting to feel stuck after receiving so many answers to prayer. From the outside looking in, no one would guess how stuck I felt. But I kept ruminating on worst-case scenarios, spiraling in fear and worry. I kept second-guessing my decision to move to Florida. I felt out of place and out of sync. My little kids were becoming big kids (the grief!), and seemingly overnight my fears went from *I hope they don't bump their heads on that table* to *I hope they don't die in a car accident.*

Oh, and the guilt. I was stuck in a murky swamp of guilt. I *should* have felt nothing but gratitude to live in a beautiful state, have my family complete, and have healthy, growing kids, but instead I was stuck feeling out of sorts, anxious, unqualified, and guilty for those feelings.

Why were my thoughts and emotions such a mess? Why couldn't I just get it together? Why couldn't my feelings cooperate and fall in line? Why didn't my body understand it was time to celebrate, not sink?

This woman's suggestion jarred me. *What exactly was she saying? Leave my family?* I was confused by her advice, which was nothing more than a hopeless suggestion. But it provoked me in the best way. It made me think about the power of choice in a way I hadn't thought of before. God used my irritation to bring me revelation.

Give up! Are you kidding me? What kind of a mom does she think I am? Do you think I'm going to up and move to Canada, live in a log cabin, and avoid my responsibilities?

But I *could* . . . That was the point.

The more I thought and prayed about it, the more I reflected on how much freedom God has given me—how much freedom God has given all of us. God gave us an enormous amount of free will. All we have to do is glance at the news and read the headlines to see all the crazy possibilities there are to exercise our free will in this one life we've been given.

At my old church in California, I served as a women's pastor for a season. I loved being present with women during life's lowest moments; it was an honor. The only person I couldn't help was a truly hopeless one. A truly hopeless person has already given up. No matter what truth I offered, no matter what solution or bit of encouragement, it was met with brick-wall energy. They claimed they'd tried everything, but nothing had worked, God wasn't coming through, and all efforts were pointless. Maybe they only needed someone to bear witness to their pain, but I often felt discouraged that I wasn't able to shift their perspective. They felt stuck, and there was nothing I could do to help.

I wondered if that was exactly the kind of brick-wall energy I brought to the worst advice giver that day. Maybe that's why she told me I could give up if I wanted to. I gave her the "I've tried everything and I'm stuck" energy, and she wanted to snap me out of it.

"Why don't you just give up?"

Somehow those words shocked me like spiritual defibrillators. They made me snap out of my hopeless cycle. They made me realize that even though I felt stuck, I did have a choice. A lot of choices, in fact.

I *could* move to Canada. Banff seems nice. I've got a passport, and the weather might be a nice change from humid Florida. I could change my identity, dye my hair, and run away from everything.

But that's not me. I'm not one who gives up on the people I love or on my God-given assignments.

So I indeed have a choice. And my choice is to stay, to love, to persevere. And now that I've made my choice, I suddenly don't feel stuck anymore; I feel strong.

If you're feeling stuck, even though you know you're on the right path, I'm here to remind you that you have a choice.

You could go back to the familiar.

You could give up.

You could run and hide.

You could take an entirely different path.

Right now you have the God-given freedom to make a million different choices.

Can I offer you a different perspective on your stuckness?

Maybe you're not stuck; maybe you're the kind of person who chooses the right path even when it's the hard path. You're the kind of person who doesn't run and hide, who doesn't give up easily, who chooses character over comfort and integrity over instant gratification.

Maybe God is using this unexpected discomfort to help you turn to him and to open more chambers of your heart so you can experience joy. Full stop.

So maybe you're not stuck. Maybe you chose a harder path. Maybe you're choosing to grow through what you go through instead of running from it. And that says something about you, my friend. You're not stuck; you're strong.

MATT'S SEASON OF BUILDING

After his job fell through, my cousin Matt asked himself a question he never gave himself permission to ask before: *What do I want to do with the rest of my life?* Matt decided that he wanted to try to find his birth parents in South Korea. It took a lot of planning, but he eventually landed a job as an English teacher with a one-year contract. On February 5, 2015, he landed in Seoul, South Korea. The minute Matt stepped off the plane, he felt like he was home. He felt a presence flow over him that made him feel like he belonged. What was supposed to be a one-year journey ended up becoming five and a half years. Matt felt deeply connected to the way of life, the people, the food, and the culture.

After his second year in South Korea, Matt located the orphanage where he spent the first three years of his life. When he was three years old, he was placed with an abusive foster family in America with ten other kids. They starved most nights and lived in a house with dirt floors, and Matt was deprived of any connection to his culture. He had so many questions; he spent years wrestling with his sense of identity, confused about the purpose in all his pain. But there he was—back where it all began, standing in front of the president of the orphanage, who was still there after all those years.

The president flipped through files and records, and to both of their surprises, Matt's picture was there. Matt had always celebrated his birthday on April 14, but the president said to him, "It looks like your actual birthday would be closer to February fifth." February 5: The same day as his arrival in South Korea. He felt the same presence wash over him again, assurance that he belonged. Matt never found his birth parents, but he knew he found his home.

Through a conversation with a local Korean, Matt realized what he was called to do and what his next step was supposed to be. He needed to go back to school and get his degree in social work to help other Korean adoptees. Matt had already met many adoptees like himself—adults coming back to Korea to try to understand their heritage and identity. It occurred to Matt that he could find purpose in his pain after all. He could help other Korean adoptees so they didn't have to struggle the way he did. There was only one big problem with this new dream: Matt would have to move back to the United States for a couple of years to complete the degree program. He had spent all his life trying to find home, and now he had to leave it.

Matt moved from Korea to Florida—just a few hours from us. One would think that moving to Korea would bring a culture shock, but it was the opposite; moving back to the States was the shock. When he landed at the airport, he stood in the terminal crying and thought to himself, *I think I made a huge mistake.* He was so tempted to turn around and go back home. It was the first of many emotional breakdowns, and he couldn't shake the feeling, *What have I done?*

Matt's schedule was incredibly rigorous. Completing his degree required late nights, early mornings, intense study, and a commitment to hard work for two years straight. Matt worked full-time during the day and spent his nights taking classes and doing homework. His schedule usually allowed for only about five hours of sleep each night during the week. His weekends were spent with sixteen-hour days studying in order to expedite the process. His military background helped; he knew how to persevere and remind himself that a two-year grind was a short chapter in the bigger story of his life and calling.

Matt was in a Season of Building. He had found his purpose, his North Star, his home, and his answer to prayer, but it didn't come without an exhausting road of diligence, grit, and persistence that would stretch him to his limits.

"How does it feel to be back?" we asked when we had Matt over for dinner one night.

Matt responded immediately. "I'm sorry if I'm not myself. I'm processing so much. It just doesn't feel right here. I feel . . . almost depressed." Then he shared how hard he was working to build the future he envisioned for himself in Korea and how much he missed the culture there and couldn't wait to be back.

I asked him, "What's helping you through this huge transition?"

Matt shared that even though this was one of the hardest transitions of his life, every time he started to feel regret or depression creep in, he remembered his end goal.

"You have to remember your why," Matt said. "My purpose to help other adoptees refuels me every time I start to think I made a huge mistake. It also reminds me that it's temporary. I count the months I have left until I can go back, and I remember that this feeling of being stuck won't last forever."

Huge life shifts, even ones you know are the right choice, can have this kind of effect on our emotions. The doubts and feelings of regret aren't anything to beat ourselves up about. They are just our bodies' way of saying, *This is hard. I really want to feel settled again.*

I recently caught up with Matt over FaceTime, and he's back in Korea once again. He completed his goal and was recently asked to speak at a convention in Seoul for Korean adoptees from around the world. With a big smile on his face, he shared how he now spends his days counseling others and working part-time as a scuba-diving instructor. Although Matt never found his birth parents, he found his purpose and he found his home.

People in a Season of Building like Matt aren't stuck; they're strong.

If you are like Matt and in a Season of Building, you are working hard in the natural to build what you prayed for in the spiritual. You have choices, but you are choosing to do what's hard in the short term for what's purpose-filled in the long term. The cement may be wet. The scaffolding may be messy. You might have tired eyes and calloused hands. But being in a Season of Building means you know that what you're enduring is forming something greater. Like Matt, when you continue to stay focused on the why behind the work, you remember that the discomfort of now is not the definition of forever. Even though on some days you probably feel broken, busted, and buried, I'm here to assure you that you're building. It's normal to feel weary when you're adjusting to a big change, building a dream brick by brick, and trying to remember that the grind you're in isn't a life sentence.

"NOW WHAT?"

Did you know there is a term for that "Now what?" feeling? As it turns out, *the arrival fallacy* (or what I like to call "Now what?" syndrome) is a term used to describe the feelings of emptiness, confusion, or disappointment people experience after reaching a major goal or milestone. It's that moment when you achieve what you've been working (or praying) for, but instead of feeling fulfilled, you find yourself stuck, thinking, *Now what? Is this all there is?*

"Now what?" syndrome can also happen when you set your sights so intently on something, you never considered what would be next. I had achieved such a big milestone in adopting children that I never considered what would come after. And for some that can feel paralyzing. Some people spend so much time, energy, and resources planning a wedding, they come back from the honeymoon with "Now what?" syndrome. This happens commonly to graduates and retirees too. Such big transitions (though positive) can leave people with a loss of purpose, depression, and even an identity crisis.

If there is a name for the arrival fallacy, then we better start talking about it. We need to normalize this experience instead of judging people (or ourselves) for our seemingly mismatched feelings. Here's a list of names you might recognize of people who may have experienced "Now what?" syndrome:

- **Adele.** Adele became a mother amid finding massive success from her hit albums *21* and *25*. Between tours and her rising popularity, she wrestled with postpartum depression and the mom guilt so many of us have become familiar with.[1]
- **Tom Brady.** After winning his third Super Bowl, Brady famously said in a *60 Minutes* interview, "Why do I have three Super Bowl rings and still think there's something greater out there for me?" He became one of the greatest quarterbacks of all time but still wrestled with a sense of emptiness.[2]
- **Michael Phelps.** After winning twenty-three Olympic gold medals for swimming, Phelps questioned what he had left to accomplish. Despite achieving immense accomplishments and reaching the pinnacle of his sport, he struggled with depression, isolation, and substance abuse.[3]
- **Jim Carrey.** In a quote shared widely across social media, the actor and comedian said, "I think everybody should get rich and famous and do everything they ever dreamed of so they can see that it's not the answer." Despite achieving enormous success, he has been open about his struggles with depression and finding deeper meaning.
- **John Lennon.** After the Beatles disbanded, Lennon admitted

he felt disillusioned by fame, saying in an interview in 1970, "The dream is over." Even at the height of success, he found that what the world called a dream sometimes felt more like an illusion.[4]

- **Jon Krakauer.** After his experience reaching the top of Mount Everest, Krakauer shared how reaching the summit felt strangely hollow and that climbing Everest had been deeply unsettling instead of fulfilling. He described feeling detached and even regretful, instead of the euphoria he expected.[5]
- **Scottie Scheffler.** Even though Scheffler was ranked number one in the world at golf, he said in an interview, "It feels like you work your whole life to celebrate winning a tournament for a few minutes. . . . At the end of the day, sometimes I just don't understand the point. . . . We work so hard for something that's so fleeting." He went on to say, "It's an unsatisfying venture. I guess what I'm trying to say is this is not the place to look for your satisfaction."[6]

Although my journey of relocating, shifting jobs, and adopting doesn't compare to winning three Super Bowls or an Olympic gold medal, I can relate to "Now what?" syndrome. There is a natural feeling of paralysis after reaching a high in life. *Psychology Today* described this as "post-achievement depression," when feelings such as purposelessness, restlessness, or fatigue are common after a milestone is reached.[7]

Whether it's retiring, adopting children, or winning a gold medal, what I've learned is that our valleys can feel like peaks with God, and our peaks can feel like valleys without God. We need God just as much in our highs as we do in our lows, and it takes strength and humility to recognize that. Once you've lived enough life, you realize what C. S. Lewis said is true: "If I find in myself a desire which no experience in this world can satisfy, the most probable explanation is that I was made for another world."[8]

RYAN'S SEASON OF BALANCING

After twenty-two years of service, my brother-in-law Ryan was finally approaching retirement from his role as an officer in the army. After countless nights sleeping on cots in the Middle East, he looked forward to sleeping in his own bed with his wife and seeing his kids every day. He dreamed of taking a year off, golfing, and eventually finding a nice worry-free nine-to-five job. He also looked forward to his retirement ceremony. It was a huge formal event—a mile marker of accomplishment for years of tremendous sacrifice and duty.

Unfortunately the arrival of Ryan's retirement came at a time of economic uncertainty. His long-anticipated retirement celebration turned into an anticlimactic (and mostly virtual) event. And his plans to take a year off and golf went out the window as his main priority was providing for his family.

Now what? he wondered.

While everyone congratulated him on his retirement and patted him on the back, he couldn't shake his anxieties about what was next.

Ryan remembered a conversation he had a year prior with his Uncle Don, a retired air force colonel.

"What are you going to do after you retire?" Don asked.

Ryan told him his exciting plans: gap year, golfing, worry-free job.

"Can I tell you my experience?" Don asked.

Don shared how he applied for a job at a nuclear power plant upon retirement. His qualifications were extensive. Even though he didn't go to space, Don was a trained astronaut with an engineering degree from MIT and a high rank as an air force colonel. The power plant affirmed that Don's résumé was impressive. But none of it mattered. They asked how many words per minute he could type and offered him an entry-level desk job. Don would have to work his way up from the bottom. He no longer had his rank or seniority and would have to re-earn people's respect as an entry-level employee.

"Just remember: You're never above anything," Don told Ryan.

Now, more than ever, Ryan needed those words.

One company finally reached out and offered Ryan a position. It wasn't an industry Ryan was interested in, it would require long hours, and it certainly didn't account for Ryan's qualifications. But it was a job, and he would be home with his family.

You're never above anything, Ryan reminded himself. He took the job and prepared for his first day.

"Business casual," the welcome email said. Those two words brought on debilitating anxiety. *What does that even mean?*

In the army every small decision is made for you. For twenty-two years Ryan's packing list was provided and his life was structured. Even though he grew accustomed to making big multimillion-dollar, lives-at-stake decisions, he didn't have to make any small ones, like what to wear. He never expected two little words in an email to make him feel so stuck: *business casual.*

Making small decisions was one of many adjustments Ryan had to make in his postretirement life. On the outside people saw a picture of a beautiful family: a husband retiring from the military and moving on to a new job. It was all good change, a huge milestone worthy of celebrating. But people don't see the "Now what?" moments behind the scenes for veterans like Ryan. From panicking about what to wear to sitting in the doctor's office wondering what happy feels like to memories popping up from the times on deployment when death was accepted as fact. Retirement was worth celebrating, but it certainly didn't feel like Ryan thought it would feel.

Even though Ryan's retirement doesn't involve a cushy job or endless tee times, the majority of the year he's home with his family—and that's what matters most to him. When I visit my sister, Ryan is either playing baseball with his son in the backyard or sitting in his favorite chair working. Our family has invited their family to go camping, but he smiles and reminds us that he's retired from the life of sleeping on cots outside.

Fair enough.

GOD IS GREATER THAN THE HILLS AND VALLEYS

God is greater than the hills and valleys. It's a truth that people write songs about and even get tattoos to showcase. But mostly people sing those lyrics or look to those tattoos as reminders of the strength of God through their valleys. After all, "God is greater than my cancer diagnosis" has more weight than "God is greater than my promotion at work."

Unfortunately it's when we are in the peak seasons of life that it's easiest to forget about God. It's second nature to cry out to God in times of desperation, but it's all too easy to forget God when we are on the mountaintop (especially if we inadvertently believed the mountaintop would satisfy us). "Now what?" syndrome is proof that no peak, bestselling book, Olympic gold medal, career milestone, or Super Bowl victory will ever bring our souls satisfaction. God is the only one big enough to fill that chasm. When we try to fill our souls with milestones and achievements, it's like trying to fill the Grand Canyon with a squirt gun. It doesn't mean we don't continue to reach for goals or pray for gifts. It means we need the constant reminder that our souls' satisfaction can never be found in the gift but only in the Giver.

One of the hardest parts about parenting is getting to the phase when your kids no longer "need" you. It's easy to confuse being *needed* with being *loved*, and it's a strange position to be in wondering if your grown child will call you that day, not because they need something but simply because they love you. I wonder if that's how God feels when we reach the peak seasons of our lives. We are no longer crying on the bathroom floor because we need God desperately. Life is good, things are happening—and God goes on the back burner. These moments in life reveal the content of our hearts. Do we really *need* God? Do we really *want* God? Do we really *love* God?

Augustine Aurelius (a.k.a. Saint Augustine) read *Hortensius*, a dialogue by the Roman philosopher Cicero that explained how everyone intends on being happy, but the majority of people are miserable, frustrated, and full of unfulfilled longings. Augustine set out to discover why most people are so discontent. At the end of his quest, he concluded that for most of us, our lives are out of order. Sin is "ultimately a lack of love, either for God or for your neighbor. He famously stated that 'The essence of sin is disordered love.' Disordered loves means that we often love less-important things more, and more-important things less than we ought to, and this wrong prioritization leads to unhappiness and disorder in our lives."[9]

God doesn't want us to forget that the same love that enveloped us in our darkest days is still there to envelop us in our brightest. The same presence and fullness of joy we received on the bathroom floor is still available to us when we feel empty on the podium. It takes spiritual maturity to recognize that if God isn't placed in the right order in our hearts, we'll feel a void no matter what season of life we are in—a hill, a valley, or somewhere in between. When we have disordered loves, we will have a disordered heart.

One of my mentors once said, "You weren't meant to live on the mountaintop, because there's no vegetation there." And that never felt more true than after I received my answers to prayer. But what I came to realize is that the reason there was no vegetation was because I lost my desperation. It took the emptiness and disorientation of my soul to drive me back to acknowledging my desperate need for God.

The first step? Honesty. It's impossible to experience breakthrough without honesty. If you insist on pretending everything's okay when you're empty inside, you'll keep feeling empty inside. And can I share another hard truth? If you constantly pretend like everything's okay in your relationships (with God or with others) when it's not, that's not a real relationship; that's an act. It might not feel safe to admit you're struggling with your new baby, your retirement, or your new dream job. But do you know who you aren't fooling? God. So stop pretending, at least with him.

When you arrive at a mall, one of the first things you do is look at the directory. The tall display shows a map of the shops, and you can scan for the yellow star labeled You Are Here. Determining your starting point is critical before you can take the first step toward your end point. Without this knowledge, you'll wander aimlessly, feeling lost and stuck.

We need to have a We Are Here moment with God: a moment when we acknowledge that our star on the map looks different on the outside than it does on the inside. A moment when we show up not as we wish we were but as we are.

God is indeed bigger than the hills and valleys, and he's also bigger than your feelings on the hills and in the valleys. He's bigger than your pretending, he's bigger than your striving, and his love is bigger than all the guilt you've carried for your complicated feelings and the wishes that you were further along.

So, what if you're not stuck, but you're strong? You're strong for not running away, but you're also strong because you will show up in your weakness and rely on his strength. This paradox is one of the great mysteries God gave us: "For when I am weak, then I am strong."*

Here's your permission slip to come to God just as you are. To admit your weakness and receive his strength. To confess that somewhere along the way, you put God in the wrong order and outsourced his job to fill your soul. Your answer to prayer was never meant to fill you; only God can do that. But you know better now, and you're ready to trade "Now what?" syndrome for the living water of his presence, the source that never runs dry. Let the lack of vegetation lead you back to desperation, and watch as God begins to revive your soul from stuck to strong.

---

* 2 Corinthians 12:10.

Pray It Through

Pray with the three *R*'s.

1. **Read:** Read through a verse once out loud.
2. **Reflect:** Repeat the verse out loud, much slower, pausing and reflecting on each phrase.
3. **Respond:** Turn the verse into a prayer.

Here are some examples you can use to get you started.

HEBREWS 13:8

Verse: "Jesus Christ is the same yesterday and today and forever."

Prayer: *God, thank you that you are the same yesterday, today, and forever. Although seasons change, you are constant.*

MATTHEW 4:4

Verse: "Bread alone will not satisfy, but true life is found in every word that constantly goes forth from God's mouth" (TPT).

Prayer: *God, thank you that a satisfying and true life is not found in my feelings, my season, or my circumstances; it's found in you and your Word.*

LUKE 1:30

Verse: "Do not yield to your fear" (TPT).

Prayer: *God, new beginnings are bringing new fears in my life. Give me the strength not to yield to those fears. I want to yield to the Holy Spirit.*

Anchor Your Soul

Get out a pen and a journal and write down the following prompts:

- The stuck story I'm telling myself is . . . (Write down all the hopeless, stuck, or limiting thoughts you've had.)
- The story of God's strength in my life is . . . (Write down the truth about God's strength as seen in Scripture and in your life.)

Chapter 6

THE BEST KIND OF CHANGE

I never have any difficulty believing in miracles, since I experienced the miracle of change in my own heart.

—SAINT AUGUSTINE

I asked my friend if she had any good worship songs she was listening to these days. She recommended a song called "Everything Is Changing." I laughed and said, "I'll have to listen to that one. That sounds like the theme of my life right now."

I expected the song to be about how change is hard but God is with you and he never changes—you know, kind of like what this book is about. But the lyrics took me by surprise. It was about how everything is changing because God entered the room. It was about how God changes people in a good way—how he redeems, restores, renews, and resurrects. I felt convicted. Somewhere along the way I'd become so bitter about all the changes I'd been through that I saw change through only one lens: hard. I'd lost sight of the best kind of change God brings: that he is the God who can reach down and change any heart, mine included.

In the last chapter I gave you a different perspective on your "stuckness" and some reasons you might feel stuck (like "Now what?" syndrome) to help you normalize your experience. I covered how when we feel stuck and weak, God gets the chance to give us his strength.

But what happens when we feel resistant to change and inward transformation? Sometimes we want God's strength and we want growth, but if we're honest, we want to know first how much it's going to cost us. C. S. Lewis said it best: "We are not necessarily doubting that God will do the best for us: we are wondering how painful the best will turn out to be."[1]

I don't know how long your transition will last before you find your footing. But I do know that we can anchor ourselves to God in ways that make us feel steady through the choppiest waters of change fatigue. We can grow through what we go through. If the very word *change* comes out of your mouth through gritted teeth, let this chapter be a reminder of the best kind of change: the kind of change where God reaches into your heart and transforms you from the inside out.

DIAPAUSE

I was in my own real-life diapause. Ever heard of one? A *diapause* is a survival mechanism in nature when development is delayed. If a creature like the caterpillar senses the conditions aren't quite right, they halt entering their chrysalis stage until the timing feels more secure. Sound familiar? *I'll grow when . . .*

the kids are out of the house.
the business is off the ground.
I'm not so busy at work.
I finish paying off debt.

We always have reasons why *now* isn't the best time to grow. Whether it's prioritizing our physical health, our mental health, our marriages, or our spiritual lives, we all have an area in our lives that we aspire to grow in but often save it for "a better time." As for me, I knew the kind of growth that was required for this season was the kind that had been in diapause for decades.

The good changes we choose and prepare for can knock us off our equilibrium and cause us to feel frozen. So it makes sense that we'd be reluctant to grow after facing a big life change. Psychologists call the state of being in transition "liminality." Scholars at INSEAD, a business school in France, and Rice University defined this as "being betwixt and between social roles and/or identities."[2] In other words, *liminality* means that you are neither in the state you left nor completely in your new state, at least not mentally. You're in the diapause.

But we aren't stuck; we are strong, remember? True. We are brave for continuing to show up in a story that feels different from what we expected. Sometimes showing up feels like all you have to give, and that's okay. But I want to invite you to wade in the water a little deeper. There's a difference between *going* through what you go through and *growing* through what you go through. If you're ready for growth, keep reading.

Facing my complicated relationship with change (a.k.a. past trauma) was not going to be easy. Like a reluctant caterpillar in its safe cocoon, I wanted to cling to the familiar. But here's the problem: Sometimes the familiar patterns stop working, the cocoon no longer feels cozy, and you watch others take flight while you're still bound.

I was clinging to my old ways, but my old ways weren't working anymore. My old schedule didn't work. My old way of praying didn't work. Neither did my old fears, my old mental pathways, my old routines. But I couldn't let go. *Why wasn't the old way working for me like it had in the past?* Maybe if I just clung harder, dug my fingers in a little deeper. But that only led to more frustration and exhaustion. The word *cling* comes from the Old English *clingan* or *clingon*, meaning "to shrink" or "to draw together." When we cling to our old ways of thinking and behaving, we are shrinking from God's best, playing small, and missing out on the transformation that comes when we surrender.

Jesus talked about how new wine needs new wineskin. A wineskin in Jesus's time was a container for wine made from animal skin (typically a goat or a sheep). Since wine ferments, the wineskin's elasticity made it perfect to hold wine as it contracted and expanded. The problem was, *old* wineskin no longer expanded; it got brittle, and if you put new wine in it, it could burst and ruin both the container and the wine. Jesus was saying that his new kingdom way of grace and transformation can't be poured into old religious systems and mindsets. And as with all of Jesus's teachings, this metaphor is pertinent to our lives today. We ask God to do something new in our lives, and he answers that prayer. He gives us new wine. But what we fail to realize is that the new wine can't be put in the old wineskin.

New life requires expansion and stretching—just ask any pregnant woman. We shouldn't pray for God to pour out something new in our lives if we have no intention of expanding anew ourselves. The new outpouring in our lives will combust into a mess if we remain inflexible, stubborn, and resistant to growth.

There's a story in the Bible about a man named Joseph who was thrown into a pit by his brothers and sold into slavery.* Through a roller coaster of trials and triumph, Joseph found himself eventually serving as second-in-command in a palace. What was most impressive wasn't the success and wealth Joseph acquired but the character transformation he underwent. At the pinnacle of his success, he met his brothers once again, and instead of retribution, he extended forgiveness and mercy. He said, "You intended to harm me, but God intended it for good to accomplish what is now being done, the saving of many lives."†

You see, Joseph didn't enter the palace with the same mindset he had in the pit. I'm afraid that many of us pray for a palace, but we can't enjoy the palace we've received because our souls are still in a hole. Your circumstances may have changed; you might have your personal definition of a palace now—family complete, white picket fence, dream job, house by the beach, dog named Spot. Check, check, check. But you still feel like the girl who could never make her mom proud, the child who had to walk on eggshells, or the kid who learned that silence was the best defense. No matter how big and beautiful your palace is, it cannot rescue your soul from a pit. And no matter how big and beautiful God is, he will not force you to surrender to a journey of inner growth and transformation. He will invite you, but he will not force you. Yielding is on you.

---

* Genesis 37–50.

† Genesis 50:20.

The walls you built up to protect yourself might be the very walls that are now keeping you imprisoned. The walls that served you in the past have now become rigid and brittle, unable to preserve the new blessings for your present and contain the ones laid out for your future. The walls of a pit and the walls of a palace are very different views, and without embarking on a journey of growth, you can't see past your past.

Well, maybe I'm just speaking for myself. It was time for me to go back so I could go forward.

UPHOLDER AND DEFENDER

If I could point to the most pivotal moment in my journey, it was in a therapist's office. I had finally surrendered to God's nudge to go to therapy—not just for a tune-up or a check-in, like I'd done a few times prior, but to face the pain of my past head-on. There's an old proverb that says, "The best time to plant a tree was twenty years ago. The second best time is now." I think the same advice applies to therapy. Should I have gone to therapy twenty years ago? Absolutely. But sometimes you're not as far along on the healing journey as you thought you were. Healing is like going up a spiral staircase. You might feel discouraged when you face the same issue again. But just because it's the same issue doesn't mean you're on the same level. As for me, I could not help my new kids heal from trauma that I hadn't healed from myself. It was time to climb to a much higher level on the staircase.

—

Tim is a sixty-six-year-old Catholic who made a career shift from a CPA to a counselor after he turned fifty. Tim is fatherly and methodical and just what I needed in my season of upheaval. After talking with Tim about all the changes I faced and how I was trying to regain my sense of balance, he set me up with a therapeutic technique that identifies false core beliefs and replaces them with new adaptive beliefs. We discussed how scary change is, especially when it feels out of your control. I did a few sessions with Tim as prep work, and then we got to the core of our work. He read an adaptive belief from a textbook: "I will focus on what I can control and surrender the rest."

Tim asked, "What do you think about that? Does that feel like a powerful truth for you?"

I thought about it for a minute and decided to be honest. "No. Not really. Maybe it's because I'm a writer and words are powerful for me. But this season of change still feels like it swallows up those little words."

Tim gave me a homework assignment to put the adaptive belief in my own words. What feels right to me? What resonates? What feels powerful? If I could anchor myself to any truth in this season, what would it be?

All week long I shuffled words in my head like a crossword puzzle, trying to find a phrase that weighed enough in my soul. At a stoplight one day, I recalled a verse that had recently stood out to me. I had written it with a Sharpie on a Post-it and stuck it on my mirror. "God is my helper; the Lord is the upholder of my life."* It was a starting point. I had also been reading about how God is our

---

* Psalm 54:4 ESV.

defender, protector, and strong fortress.* My statement of truth was starting to become my own.

The next time I met with Tim, I was ready. We shuffled through memories like a Rolodex—times when I experienced abrupt changes, times when I felt out of control. I sifted through my parents' divorce, my mom's addiction, her death, my grandma's death, and the economic crash after giving birth to my first baby. Then we moved to recent life transitions: the move, the new kids, the new job, and some shifts in relationships.

Tim said, "Now it's time to transition to your new adaptive belief. Did you come up with one?"

I nodded.

"Say it out loud," he said.

I spoke it intentionally, deliberately, not missing one syllable of one word.

"God is the upholder of my life and the defender of my heart."

The moment those words came out of my mouth, I was afraid to move a muscle, because I didn't want to interrupt what I was experiencing. I was enveloped by a presence of comfort, assurance, peace, confidence, and love.

I've heard people share how small they've felt in God's presence. But strangely, instead of feeling smaller, I felt bigger. Maybe it's because God knew I had already felt cut down to size; I already felt small and humbled and helpless, swept into a tornado of change and unable to find my way out. But in this moment I felt powerful and anchored and whole. I felt God big within me. It was as if I had been a little girl bullied on the playground, but in this moment my Father stood up and towered over it all.

* Psalm 18:1–2, 84:9–10.

His presence was powerful and authoritative, and I understood that I carried that same power and authority. First John 4:4 felt personal now: "Greater is He who is in you than he who is in the world" (NASB).

Tears rolled uncontrollably down my face. Through all these changes in my life, I'd felt powerless. But not now. Now I was wrapped up with an unshakable strength. My Father was in the room.

"Now take a deep breath," Tim prompted. "Say it again."

I let the air fill my lungs slowly. I felt the expansion of my diaphragm, my feet firmly planted on the ground. I held my head high as if I had a microphone and an audience in front of me. Again I spoke my truth out loud, uttering every word with intention.

"God is the upholder of my life and the defender of my heart."

Tim told me to take another deep breath, and with my eyes closed, I inhaled and exhaled every word as I repeated my adaptive belief in my head.

God is the upholder of my life and the defender of my heart.

God is the upholder of my life and the defender of my heart.

God is the upholder of my life and the defender of my heart.

"What's coming up for you?" Tim asked.

I had so much to say, but I didn't want to mess up this holy moment. The buzzing feeling of love and strength persisted. And as if it was downloaded into my brain, I understood with complete clarity that I get to choose how I show up in the world. It seems like a basic concept, but I felt it in my bones: I get to choose what to believe, I get to choose how I want to respond, I get to choose the kind of person I want to become, I get to choose who I want to be. Through all of life's changes, I still get to choose the kind of person I want to be. When life feels foreign and out of control, this was something no one could take from me.

Holocaust survivor Viktor E. Frankl wrote, "Everything can be taken from a man but one thing: the last of the human freedoms—to choose one's attitude in any given set of circumstances, to choose one's own way."[3] I remembered reading this quote in *Man's Search for Meaning*, but now? Now I felt the truth embodied.

I carefully raised my hands to my chest as if cherishing a precious gift. My upholder. My defender. I get to choose. I held my new truths close, like precious gems I wanted to keep gazing at forever. But mostly I didn't want the feeling to end.

Tears still rolling, I finally answered Tim's question about what was coming up for me. I couldn't utter many words. I simply said, "I just feel God so near."

And Mr. Tim, my Catholic-accountant-turned-therapist, said, "I do too. As soon as you spoke those words out loud . . . I felt him too."

SMALL GROWTH DOESN'T STAY SMALL

Maybe you don't see my moment in the therapist's office as much of a miracle. That's okay. I know how much shifted in my heart and soul that day. And here's what I've learned about growth: Even if you feel you've only grown a speck, God can do a lot with a little. Jim Forest said it this way: "A tiny seed, a small measure of yeast, a pinch of salt, a spark of light in the darkness—tiny things are capable of vast expansion and a transforming effect."[4]

Jesus said the kingdom of God is like a mustard seed—"the smallest of all the seeds on earth." But it doesn't stay small. "When it is sown it grows up and becomes larger than all the garden plants and puts out large branches, so that the birds of the air can make nests in its shade."* Jesus models this mustard-seed way by focusing on one person at a time, one healing at a time, one sermon at a time, one region at a time. He didn't say the kingdom of God was an ethereal, afterlife kind of thing—he said the kingdom is here and now, and it keeps growing. And most of the time, the growth is so gradual you barely even notice it in the day-to-day. Occasionally I wake up to its power, like when I do a double take when I notice how tall one of my children is. I see them every day and know they are growing, but some days it hits me out of nowhere. Suddenly they are not my babies anymore. It all happens so gradually and yet so fast. And so it is with our own growth and expansion. There are days when we can chart our growth like the parent drawing a pencil line on the wall, and there are other days when it feels difficult to measure.

The century plant is a perfect example of why we can't discount small growth or slow growth. The common name arose because it was once thought to take one hundred years for the plant to flower. (We now know that number is closer to ten to twenty-five years, but it's still a long time.) This six-foot plant is a survivor, tolerating droughts for long periods. It spends years holding back its fruit and potential. But once the plant decides it's time to shine, it shoots up like a telephone pole, growing quickly to twenty or thirty feet tall. The flower structure resembles a candelabrum sitting atop a stalk. After it blooms, it's unrecognizable, looking more like a beautiful tree than a simple desert plant.

Scripture encourages us to let our roots grow down into God and let our lives be built on him so that our faith grows strong.† It doesn't say whether it will be a gradual growth, growth spurts, or

* Mark 4:30–32 ESV.

† Colossians 2:6–7.

growth that lies low for years, then shoots up like the century plant. But it does say that when we are rooted in him, we will grow strong. Exponential changes hold the potential for exponential growth, like a century plant blooming. And although most of my growth felt like the slow mustard-seed kind, that moment in Tim's office was my century-plant moment.

Do you know what strong trees need to develop strong roots? It turns out they need shifting seasons—or at a minimum, shifting weather. The Biosphere 2 experiment in the 1990s tried to re-create optimal Earth conditions artificially (you know, in case an apocalypse forces us to live in space). For several reasons the experiment failed. But one of the reasons was that they couldn't re-create wind in such a perfectly controlled environment. As a result the trees grew quickly but kept falling over. Without gentle breezes and fierce storms, the trees couldn't develop a strong root system.[5] It's through the endurance of shifting seasons and shifting weather that century plants can tower.

As much as we may resist (and even at times despise) the torrent of shifting seasons in our lives, we can't deny they serve a purpose. Enduring through every season builds strong roots. It grows us in ways that perfectly curated conditions cannot.

Even if we can't see it right now, we will look back and be able to spot the growth. Researcher and author of *Life Is in the Transitions*, Bruce Feiler, found that 90 percent of the time, the people he studied and spoke with judged their transitions as successes; the transition ended, and they found themselves once again on solid ground.[6] Even better, research shows that we tend to see past events—even unwanted ones—as net positives over time. Though our brains tend to focus on negative emotions in the present, over the years unpleasant feelings fade more than pleasant feelings do, a phenomenon known as "fading affect bias." Almost every transition—even the most challenging ones—bears some positive fruit; it just takes time to see and feel its effects.[7]

Your growth might start small, but it doesn't stay small. Let your roots grow down into God; he will sustain and strengthen you through every changing season. It might take longer than you want, but you will see the fruit of your perseverance. You will grow, you will mature, and your faith will be strengthened.

NEW GROWTH IS HERE—CAN YOU SEE IT?

A small but desperate "Help!" is all I heard before I tossed, without thinking, the barbecue spatula on the grill to run over to my son lying in the yard.

My oldest son is one of the most agile kids in the world. Even from a young age, he made other moms gasp as he spider-monkeyed his way up jungle gyms, trees, walls—whatever was in sight. I always shrugged it off—just another day in the life with my daredevil child. He never got hurt, so I suppose I started to view him as invincible.

As we all rushed over to him, the L shape of his forearm became clear. The echoes of my girls' screaming filled my yard and my home. He had been swinging on a palm-tree branch in our backyard. The branch snapped, and his entire body weight landed on his forearm, snapping both forearm bones in half.

The whole experience sends a stinging feeling down my spine

when I remember it—the look on his face, the deformed arm, the excruciating pain, and the way his eyes rolled back in his head when the doctor gave him ketamine before resetting the bones. I'm still not sure why they allowed me to be in the room. My husband, queasy and overwhelmed, opted out.

We came home from the hospital late that night, and my spatula lay charred and melted into the grill. My son needed to sleep in my husband's and my room for a while: The medicine made him loopy, and he needed to stay stationary until they could put a real cast on his arm. The doctor made it clear: If those bones moved even slightly, his arm would require surgery.

After my son had been in a cast for a couple of months, I took him to his orthopedic appointment to see if it was time to remove it. They took new X-rays, and when the doctor pulled them up on the screen, my heart sank. I could still clearly see the brokenness. Was his arm not healing? Would he need surgery? I felt my cheeks flush and my body grow hot as I anticipated bad news.

The doctor said, "Look at this! This looks fantastic! Look at all that new growth!"

I wondered if we were looking at the same image. But the doctor began pointing out spots on the X-ray that my eyes weren't trained to see, spots where new bone was growing around the break.

"Do you see that? Do you see the growth?" he said enthusiastically.

Truthfully, I could barely make it out. The jagged lines of the break were much more pronounced than the new growth. But as the doctor traced his finger along faint lines, I began to see what he was talking about. What appeared slight to me seemed significant to the expert.

He said, "With all that new growth, that arm is going to be even stronger than it was before."

I know kids break bones all the time, but this was my first experience with anything other than a hairline fracture. *Do broken bones heal stronger than before? Is that a thing?* I couldn't believe what I was hearing. And something hit me at that moment. If God can do that with a broken bone, what could he do with a broken heart? A discouraged spirit? A soul that feels displaced?

Sometimes when we experience change fatigue, all we can see is the pronounced brokenness—the ways we haven't adapted, the ways we've resisted, the struggles we've carried. Our eyes haven't yet been trained to spot the character forming. But God, with his higher perspective, views our brokenness differently. While our perspective might be, "Look at all that brokenness," God's perspective is, "Look at all that new growth!"

If all we focus on is the brokenness, our eyes never get trained with a higher perspective. That's why gratitude is powerful; it forces us to play a game of I spy with the goodness in our lives. The most beautiful truth washed over me as I stared at the X-ray and listened to the doctor: God can take the shattered areas of our lives and make them stronger than before. Our weakest point can become a strength.

The new growth is there, even in our most broken season. Do you see it?

Surrendering to the process of growth takes courage, and spotting growth along the way takes intentionality. Both are important, because spotting and celebrating your growth (no matter how small) will fuel you to keep growing. And before you know it, your speck of a seed (that could easily blow away by the winds of change) becomes a sturdy and unshakable tree.

Pray It Through

God, I thank you that you invite me to grow through what I go through. Thank you that you invite me to become more like you. Change me during this season of change. Transform me, make me more like you, and reveal new truths that will help me reframe my past and step into wholeness. Amen.

Anchor Your Soul

Write down a word that describes exactly how you want to show up in this new season. Think about a time when you embodied that quality well. Sit with that image for a minute, remembering how it felt to show up in a way you were proud of. Pray that God would continue to grow that quality in you daily and make you more like him.

Now write on a sticky note, "I am becoming more ________ [your word] every day because of Christ" and put it on your mirror or somewhere you will see it often. If your word was patient, then your sentence becomes, "I am becoming more patient every day because of Christ."

Chapter 7

NEW BEGINNINGS

When one door of happiness closes,
another opens; but often we look so long
at the closed door that we do not see the
one which has been opened for us.

—HELEN KELLER

The best thing about living in Florida is the ability to take plenty of trips to the beach. In the summer I like to swim in the ocean, but most months, my favorite thing to do is sit in my beach chair, read a good book, and watch my kids build sandcastles (or sand snowmen). They don't do it as much now that they are older, but they used to find sticks, seashells, grass, and other trinkets to decorate their sand creations. They knew the tide was creeping in, and as the water inched closer to their creations, they tried to build a sand barrier to protect them. Their smiles grew bigger with the thrill of each new, sneaky wave. How long would their creations last? It became a game.

My kids were never devastated when their sandcastles got swept away; they knew the tide was coming, and their creations weren't meant to be permanent. They embraced the tide's destructive force with a playful attitude. They dusted the sand off their shorts and relocated to a new creative spot. I envied their mindsets—hearts free from the fear of losing what they'd invested their time into, no reservations about starting over and building something new.

I wish I shared my children's ability to shift and glide from one thing to the next. I grow sentimental about letting go of each season of life, sometimes in nonsensical ways. When it comes to the waves of change, somewhere along the way I lost my playful attitude. I lost the ability to see the tides of change as fun or as an exciting new beginning; I only saw them as a threat to destroy what I've worked so hard to build. Scripture makes a clear distinction between the temporal and the eternal: "The grass withers, the flower fades, but the word of our God will stand forever."* Yet somehow this doesn't stop me from getting too attached to the sandcastles in life. Corrie ten Boom said, "I must learn to hold earthly things lightly because if I do not the Lord might have to pry away my fingers, and that hurts."[1]

Maybe you can relate to tight-fisting your way through life.

Maybe, like me, you're having trouble letting go of the way things used to be before everything changed.

What would it feel like to hold the sand a little softer?

What would it look like to welcome the tides of change with more childlike wonder?

---

* Isaiah 40:8 ESV.

What if we perceived transitions as new possibilities rather than losses?

My children released sandcastles to the waves the way I want to release seasons to God. They didn't focus on what they'd lost, because there was an expanse of untouched sand ready for constructing and creating. Their eyes sparked with creativity while their hands dug again, full of new sand and new possibilities.

Isn't that what we all want? To see our new beginnings as new blessings, to see them with fresh eyes and fresh hearts. I wonder how often we're missing out on the full joy of our current season because we're too busy looking back on the last one. Are we missing out on creating new memories because we're pining over old ones? What a gift it is to let the waves wash over what was created in one season and be able to anticipate and celebrate the new one. But how do we get there?

In this chapter I'm going to help you grab a shovel and find the courage to dig again. You may feel like you've lost your energy, wonder, spark, and creativity. You may feel like you expected a castle, but all you have is a pile of sand with more waves on the horizon. I'm going to help you see your season with fresh, new eyes. This season and this day are full of promise. Let's take back our childlike wonder one handful of sand at a time.

A NEW BEGINNING FOR YOUR NEW BEGINNING

It's hard to savor the newborn stage when your baby cries for hours, sleep comes in broken fragments, and you second-guess every decision.

It's hard to enjoy a new job when every task feels unfamiliar, you're still finding your footing, and you miss the confidence that came so easily in your old role.

It's hard to relish being a newlywed when you realize love doesn't mean that communication comes naturally, your differences feel like deadlocks, and the closeness you hoped for takes more work than you imagined.

When you show up in a story that feels different from what you expected, you get tired of running into the same wall of disenchantment. You keep beating yourself up for not entering this new story with more joy or gratitude or whatever it is you thought you would feel. But what if you let that old story go? The one that you keep wrestling with, the one full of expectations. What if you decided to embrace a new beginning? You might be thinking, *I already have a new beginning—a hard one too. What more do you want?* Here's what I mean: You need a new beginning in the way you approach your new beginning. You need to reenter your story with a new lens. This time, without all the expectations of how your story would look or feel.

In Isaiah 43:19 God said, "See, I am doing a new thing! . . . do you not perceive it?" God could have left that last part out. He could have announced he was doing a new thing. But God knows our human nature; he knows we often don't *perceive* it. Jesus spoke about those who could understand his parables when he said, "Blessed are your eyes because they see, and your ears because they hear."*

God already gave us a new beginning. We are in a new season, living in an answer to our prayers. The problem isn't that we're

* Matthew 13:16.

awaiting the new chapter; it's that we're having trouble perceiving it from God's perspective. Life is always about perspective.

Sometimes the first step in enjoying your new story is letting the old one go. If you're still living in the land of disappointment and unmet expectations, it's time to let that old story go the way my kids let go of their sandcastles. It's time to let the tide wash away your presupposed timelines. It's time to let go of the limits and labels you've placed on yourself. Let the old narrative go that says you would be happy if you could only go back to the way things were before (mindset check: Just because it could have been different doesn't mean it would be better). Let go of the old framework, the old plot, the old pace. Let that story wash out with the tide. Let go of the last chapter of your life and decide to look back on it with only gratitude, not with rose-colored lenses or unhealthy nostalgia. Let go of expectations and regrets and coulda, shoulda, wouldas.

A wise counselor once said to me, "There's a reason the windshield is bigger than the rearview mirror. It's better to focus on the future than dwell on the past. But do you know what's even bigger than the windshield? The inside of the car. It's important to be where your feet are." She gave me this advice because she knows I'm the type of person who gets stuck staring into the rearview mirror.

Only when you take the brave step of letting go of the past and your unmet expectations about the present can you move toward accepting your reality and realigning your heart. Your new beginning deserves a new beginning. But you won't be able to perceive the new thing God is doing if you don't let go and accept your reality.

This is it. This is the life you've got. With all its complexity and chaos and layers, this is your one life. It might not be what you expected it to be, but that doesn't mean it isn't a gift or that you can't find a new way to enter your story. If the front door is locked, crawl in through the window—but by all means, find a way to reenter your story with fresh eyes.

When I was in my most disoriented state, I could only dream of being settled, stable, and steady. I only wanted to find my footing again. That was it. Eventually God prompted me to dream beyond steady and settled. There were new beginnings for me on the horizon that he wanted to show me. But there were limiting beliefs, mindsets, and filters clouding my vision.

So how do we see our stories with fresh eyes? What does that look like practically? Here's a start:

1. **Identify your unmet expectations.** Revisit chapter 2 and make a list of all the high hopes and expectations you had when you were praying for the life you have today. What disappointments are you facing? What unexpected emotions are weighing you down? What curveballs were you thrown? Write all of it down without judging or editing your words.
2. **Identify unhealthy nostalgia.** Next write down any areas where you might be clinging to the old sandcastles in life—previous seasons that you might be looking at with rose-colored lenses. In what ways are you getting stuck looking in the rearview mirror? How is pining over the past holding you back from enjoying the present? Write down ways that you've slipped into unhealthy nostalgia.
3. **Accept your reality.** I know, this is a hard one. Acceptance is not easy. In his book *The Gifts of Acceptance*, Daniel Miller said, "Until you are able to stop trying to change what you are powerless over, you will not be able to clearly see the

constructive steps you can take to adapt to it."[2] What is the current reality you are living in? Not the life you wish you had, not the life you used to have, but what is your current situation that you need to accept? Write down the truth about your circumstances and emotions, the good, the bad, and the ugly. Now in two separate columns, write down everything that's within your control and everything that's outside of your control.

4. **Ask God to help you perceive what he's doing.** Take time to release any unmet expectations of the present or unhealthy nostalgia to God. Ask him to help you expect his goodness while accepting his way of bringing it. Ask him to help you have fresh eyes to see the new thing he is doing in your life. Pray, *God, help me have a new beginning for my new beginning. Help me perceive what you're doing in my life.*

This is gritty work, but it's also holy. Remember, as believers we need to learn to expect the loving-kindness of God without writing ourselves a prescription for exactly what it looks like. We need to learn how to be people who hold the sandcastles in life loosely. If we don't, we will miss out on the joy of creating something new. Here's to new beginnings.

DON'T STEP IN THE KITCHEN

After the adoption the energy in my home shifted. Three kids is a group, but five kids is a party. Most parents take four months and twenty-three days to feel adjusted to life with a newborn baby (I did not adjust that fast), but I have yet to find data on the adjustment period for adopting a sibling set from foster care.[3] All I know is that it felt like a blur, and I wasn't sure when I'd find solid ground again. It was going to be a while before the inside of my four walls felt the same, and as a homebody who likes to recharge on the couch with a good book, I wasn't sure how (or where) to recharge anymore. What happens when your peaceful place becomes the party place? I knew something needed to change. When a friend suggested pickleball, my brain drifted. *Not for me. I don't do hobbies that force me out of the house.* But then the thought hit me: *What if a hobby outside of the home is exactly what I need in this season? How far out of my comfort zone am I willing to travel to recharge?*

John Maxwell said, "If you're growing you're always going to be out of your comfort zone."[4] Quotes like this feel inspirational when you're reading them on a poster hanging in the doctor's office, but here's the honest truth: It feels like eating grass when you put them into practice.

There's nothing more uncomfortable and awkward than trying something new, especially by yourself. Yep, I showed up to the pickleball courts by myself. My husband and I had opposite schedules, and I didn't know anyone else who played in the evenings, so I showed up at Halpatiokee Regional Park with a paddle and a confused look on my face. I felt like a middle schooler trying to find someone to sit with at lunch. And when I jumped into my first game, I was terrible. I didn't understand why everyone kept telling me to get out of the kitchen. *Kitchen? Do I look like the only thing I'm good for is cooking? Like a woman who is supposed to be barefoot and pregnant in the kitchen? Is this some kind of sexist joke?*

I came home covered in sweat and mosquito bites, annoyed, and with a pit in my stomach that I hadn't felt in years. I felt embarrassed and gawky, and I hated the idea of subjecting myself to any more feelings of ineptitude. I did not want to go back. But as I showered that night, I remembered the advice I always give my kids when they start something new: "Be brave enough to be the worst one at first." (Dang it! It is so much easier giving advice than taking it.) Then another thought hit me: *Maybe this is what growth feels like.*

I put pickleball on my calendar for Monday and Wednesday nights. It was my new nonnegotiable. I was going to take my own advice to be brave enough to be the worst and embrace being uncomfortable and awkward. But first I needed to sign up for lessons, because I really frustrated other players over this kitchen thing. During my last game a surfer-looking dude who goes by the name Rooster said, "Girl, you weren't just in the kitchen. You were flipping pancakes." I thought I was on a pickleball court playing pickleball, but okay.

At my first pickleball lesson, my coach explained that you can't step in "the kitchen" (the section near the net) if you're hitting the ball out of the air before it bounces. I was relieved to learn it wasn't a sexist joke. My coach drilled me to keep my feet firmly planted next to the kitchen line (but not over it) while he fed me balls to hit out of the air. The idea was to get used to my feet being immovable. No matter what came my way, my feet could not go over that line. I had to remain firmly planted. Drill after drill after drill. My muscle memory began to form.

We ran the same drills week after week. Slowly, I started to get better, and the awkwardness on the court began to fade. (And look at me now—I have a hobby outside the home I enjoy. Who would have thought?) Playing pickleball became a snapshot of how I felt during my season of change fatigue. I was showing up even while I was clumsy, uncomfortable, and full of knots in my stomach. I was letting go of the old story that I'm an introverted homebody. Not anymore. *This is what growth feels like,* I'd tell myself. I was learning how to accept my reality and let go of my expectations and things outside of my control. *This is what growth feels like.* I was learning how to ask God to help me perceive what he was doing in my life (instead of constantly comparing it to what he had done in the past). *This is what growth feels like.* I was failing, but I was failing forward. I was doing it all wrong a little less each day, developing a rhythm of surrender even when it hurt. *This is what growth feels like.*

I wish I could tell you that it was all fun, but I said it before and I'll say it again: Getting out of your comfort zone, growing, and embracing a new beginning feels like eating grass at first. Grass with dirt mixed in. I don't share that to discourage you. I share it so that when you wake up in the morning and make difficult decisions, you'll know they are just that: difficult. Surrendering, letting go, releasing your expectations, accepting your reality, growing, forgiving, healing, stretching yourself—these things weren't meant to be easy. The good news is, the grass-eating feeling gets better after a while, and the reward is more than worth it. And the even better news? You aren't doing it alone. God is right there with you, offering his strength, enablement, and higher perspective.

Every time I stood at the kitchen line, I remembered how those drills with my coach related to transitions. Changes in life will come at us, one after another, but they all serve one purpose: to train us to keep our feet planted in God. Everything else will shift, so we need a firm foundation. Jesus described following him as being like a wise man who built his house on the rock rather than on shifting sand. The house with a rock foundation stood against the winds, rain, and floods, but the one built on the sand did not.*

---

* Matthew 7:24–27.

Building a house on the sand seems tempting. Who doesn't want a waterfront view? But a structure on a shifting foundation never holds up. We need something steady and fixed to build our lives upon. When we live our lives with this firm foundation, the tides of change don't shake us like they used to. We know what's firm and steady under our feet. We know that God is not going to run short on new ways to bless us in our new season. But there's the digging part, the building part—the part that feels like eating grass—that we have to embrace in order to see something new begin to form in our lives.

A LOT CAN CHANGE IN A DAY

A coworker of mine opened up about suffering from postpartum depression after she gave birth to her firstborn. She was overwhelmed with gratitude for her healthy baby but struggled with panic attacks, anxiety, and irrational fears of dying. She lost chunks of her hair and would often cry uncontrollably. Since she spoke of her postpartum depression in past tense, I asked her what helped her get better. She said, "I don't know. After several months I guess my hormones finally leveled out. I just woke up one day and felt like myself again. A lot can change in a day." Although her experience is only *one* experience and doesn't represent all postpartum depression cases (I've known other women with a much longer and harder road to healing), her words struck a chord of encouragement within me: A lot can change in a day.

One day I lived in California, and the next day I lived in Florida.

One day I had three kids, and the next day I had five.

One day I was a stay-at-home mom, and the next day I worked full-time.

One day I had my footing, and the next I felt like I was dancing offbeat.

But also, if this was the case, maybe there was another "one day" waiting for me on the horizon like there was for my friend. Maybe one day I, too, would wake up and feel like myself again.

I'm guessing there are a lot of one days in your life too—before and afters that marked your life forever. Maybe the reason you're reading this book is because of one of those one days that you're still adjusting to. One day you felt like you had it all together, and the next day you felt completely disoriented. One day you were excited for the next step, and the next day you wondered if you made a big mistake.

As dramatic and overwhelming as our one days seem, we can often overlook the fact that sometimes one days come so quietly and subtly that we realize their power only in retrospect. I don't think my postpartum friend woke up knowing that *one* day was going to mark the rest of her days moving forward. I don't think she realized that one day was her new beginning. Sometimes it's only when we look back that we realize our one day came, our unassuming new beginning snuck right in and marked the start of a new chapter.

One day can bring a whole lot of overwhelm, grief, and angst, but one day can also bring peace, stability, and a fresh perspective. Henri Nouwen said, "We must learn to live each day, each hour, yes, each minute as a new beginning, as a unique opportunity to make everything new. Imagine that we could live each moment as a moment pregnant with new life. Imagine that we could live each day as a day full of promises. Imagine that we could walk through the new year always listening to a voice saying to us: 'I have a gift for you and can't wait for you to see it!'"[5]

"A lot can change in a day" became a phrase I started to say often after my conversation with my coworker. I was learning how to expect God's loving-kindness without putting so many parameters around it. If God could bring a one day to my coworker, surely God had a one day for me too. I wasn't sure when it would come or what it would look like, but I wanted to see each day as pregnant with new life, full of promise and hope, because anything is possible with God.

Consider the many one days in Scripture:

> One day Joseph was in prison, and the next he was in a palace.*
> One day David was tending sheep, and the next he was being anointed as king.†
> One day Paul was persecuting Christians, and the next he was encountering Christ.‡
> One day Jesus was dead and all hope seemed lost, and the next he resurrected and the world was never the same.§

A lot can change in a day.

One day you can wake up and feel like yourself again.

One day you can wake up and realize all the regrets and guilt are gone.

One day you can wake up and discover that you're not overwhelmed anymore.

---

* Genesis 41.
† 1 Samuel 16:1–13.
‡ Acts 9:1–5.
§ Luke 24.

One day you can wake up and realize you've found a good rhythm.

One day you can wake up and discover your inner war is over.

One day you can wake up and uncover new levels of freedom and joy in your new chapter.

One day can quietly sneak up, never announce its arrival, and tiptoe over to close the door on pain. You didn't realize it arrived until after it was gone. But that one day marked a new beginning.

A lot can change in a day.

THE HAPPY CAMPER

Although her life change was not a good or welcome change, my grandma models the principles of accepting and adapting better than anyone I know. For over a decade my grandma (a.k.a. Gigi) cared for my grandpa after his Parkinson's diagnosis. She managed everything from medication to doctors' visits to unpredictable, sleepless nights. After Grandpa went to be with Jesus in 2020, Gigi slept fourteen hours a day for seven weeks straight—her sister calling each day to make sure she was still alive.

Gigi grieved the loss of her husband and an amazing man, and in time she asked herself what she wanted to do with the rest of her life. When she decided she wanted to travel, the trip-planning process sparked a new joy in her. There wasn't a clear end date to her grieving—grief never works like that. But she decided to put one foot in front of the other and welcome happiness, even if some days still feel hard. She took me to Alaska—one of Grandpa's favorite fishing spots—and made me join her on the world's tallest zip line. Then she rode a train across Canada and saw the northern lights in Iceland (and discovered "I hope you get lucky tonight" means something different over there). Now she's got trips planned to Hawaii and Portugal.

One day I got a message from Gigi saying she'd be in my area for a couple of days because she was buying a camper to take across the country. She pulled up to my house in what looked like an aquarium—a trailer wrapped like a party bus. She named it Happy fittingly. She said, "I know Grandpa is rolling in his grave laughing about this!" Gigi's taking her Happy Camper on an epic cross-country adventure, stopping to see the Silos in Waco, the Grand Canyon, the Pioneer Woman Mercantile, and more.

During Gigi's visit I happened to be reading a book called *The Sacrament of Happy*. In the book Lisa Harper put words to what so many of us wonder: *Does God want me to be happy?* Lisa used to think that happiness and holiness were divergent paths. But the more research she did, the more she unveiled the thirty-seven references to *happy* in the Old Testament and forty-eight in the New. To boil it down: Happy and holy are not mutually exclusive, and neither are happy and sad. More accurately, happy and holy are two sides of the same coin. "Even in laughter the heart may ache."*

Harper said, "Real, God-imbued happiness is not the absence of sadness or badness. Rather, it is hanging on to the truth of His sovereign goodness regardless of what's going on within or around us."[6]

If you're anything like me, you like definitive beginnings and endings—but sometimes hard emotions and grief don't have clear finish lines. I've found myself waiting for permission to close the door on hard and open the door to happy. Here's the truth: Most

---

* Proverbs 14:13.

of the time there's no departure or arrival date. You can still miss your old life while working toward loving your new one. Sometimes you find your happy after the hard, but sometimes you learn to find happy in the hard. Sometimes the lines between hard and happy blur together, and you have to take both sides of the coin. A day when grief pops up doesn't mean you can't be happy, and hard days don't disqualify you from welcoming joy and a new beginning—even if it's found in the small things. So if you're waiting for permission to allow happiness back in, here it is from Gigi. Go get your Happy.

Lysa TerKeurst once said in a Facebook post something that has stuck with me: "Grief is a circle. Inside the rounded edges is where we go to work on accepting what will never be. Outside the edges is where a life still full of possibility exists. New joy is found when the circle is incorporated as a part of our landscape."

Here's what Gigi embodies so well: You can accept the truth about your emotions, disappointment, grief, unmet expectations, and what will never be, *and* you can adapt. You can dream again and find new joy and new possibilities. You can honor the past and move forward anyway. You can take the whole circle, the gratitude and the grief, the happy and the hard, the "what will never be" and the "what could be." You can rewrite your story and create new surprises in the plotline. Pickleball sure surprised me. And because I learned to let go and adapt, I've discovered new beginnings and new versions of myself that I didn't know existed. I enjoy learning about the stock market now (what?), I got my first tattoo (said I'd never get one), I got second place in a pickleball tournament with my husband, and I rode the world's longest zip line in Alaska (even though I'm afraid of heights). *Who. Am. I?*

It turns out I am someone who simply needed to explore the

other side of the circle. I needed to have a hobby and interests outside of motherhood and all the other changes that felt all-consuming. What I've learned from Gigi is that happiness in your new season can take on a completely different shape than the season before it. Because life is always changing, sometimes the best thing to do is change right along with it. You don't have to change who you are at your core, but you can get yourself a Happy Camper, a pickleball paddle, or a new hobby and find your new beginning one step out of your comfort zone at a time.

Pray It Through

God, thank you for all that you are teaching me in this season. Help me to perceive what you are doing in my life. Help me to let go of any expectations and unhealthy nostalgia that might be preventing me from moving forward. Give me the ability to accept my reality but the faith to expect your loving-kindness, even if it looks different from what I imagined. Give me eyes to see and ears to hear all the new possibilities that you want to show me. Amen.

Anchor Your Soul

Make a list of all the new possibilities in front of you. Now in a separate column, make a list of all the ways you are learning and growing because of your new change. In a third column make a list of how you might add value to others' lives based on your new possibilities and new insights.

NEW POSSIBILITIES	NEW GROWTH	HOW I CAN ADD VALUE

Chapter 8

IF PRAYER GOT YOU HERE . . .

How would it change your prayer life to bring to God what is actually in you and not what you think ought to be in you?

— PETER SCAZZERO

Does prayer even work?

The thought ran through my head at 11:58 p.m. during another sleepless night of change fatigue. My deep passion and love for prayer did not make me exempt from doubt. I knew that prayer worked in *some* way. After all, I got what I prayed for. But as I wrestled with complicated emotions in prayer again and again, I was left with questions:

God, why do I still feel anger sometimes?

God, why is anxiety living in my chest today?
God, why can't I stop beating myself up?

What I've realized is that prayer does work; it just doesn't always work the way I expect it to work. Prayer is not a dandelion that allows me to blow all my emotions away in one breath. Emotions don't like taking shortcuts, unfortunately. The word *emotion* comes from the Latin word *emovere*, meaning "to move through" or "to move out." Emotions are energy in motion—or at least they are supposed to be anyway. But many of us resist, deny, numb, or suppress our emotions and wonder why they keep popping up like a beach ball we've tried over and over again to submerge in water.

Prayer was not meant to take our emotions away, because God created our emotions. In fact, Jesus had all the same emotions we have. Biblical scholars identify thirty-nine different emotions Jesus had and expressed in Scripture alone. How did Jesus respond to them? He didn't ignore, repress, or numb. He turned to the Father. When Jesus was praying in the garden of Gethsemane before enduring the cross, his emotions didn't disappear. They were so intense that Scripture doesn't hold back sharing this little fact: "Being in anguish, he prayed more earnestly, and his sweat was like drops of blood falling to the ground."* The Greek word for *anguish* here is *agonia*, which means "intense struggle," "agony," or "severe mental and emotional stress." Jesus knew he was about to face betrayal, torture, and the weight of the world's sin. He didn't try to suck it up or emotionally detach. He was fully God and fully human, and he felt it all deeply.

What Jesus experienced in sweating drops of blood was a rare

---

* Luke 22:44.

condition called *hematidrosis*, where tiny blood vessels under the skin rupture due to extreme stress, causing blood to mix with sweat. Jesus modeled that it's okay to feel deeply and still run to the Father in prayer. His emotional intensity in Gethsemane shows us that emotions are not weakness; they're part of being fully human and spiritually alive.

I remember in one of my first therapy sessions I said, "I just want to warn you, I am a fruit basket of emotions. A big, colorful fruit basket." I didn't mean it in a good way; I felt ashamed of my emotions. Years later I can laugh at that moment, because I don't feel that way now. I'm human—just like everyone else. I was created with a full spectrum of emotions—just like everyone else. At the time, I didn't know my emotions were supposed to be "in motion." I didn't know how to acknowledge them honestly or process them fully. So when it came to my emotions, I felt like the Chiquita banana lady with a fruit-bowl headpiece—the fruit was mismatched and rolling around all over the place. And that made me feel out of control and ashamed (which added more fruit to my fruit basket). I've come a long way.

So if prayer doesn't instantly take our emotions away, what role does it play in helping us process our feelings around change fatigue? And how do we shift our prayer life when our new season looks different from our expectations? Maybe your once peaceful prayer spot has been replaced by tireless attempts to nurse your baby. Or your previous schedule that allowed you to connect with God effortlessly now feels like a distant memory. Or maybe getting what you prayed for was so disenchanting, you don't even know what to pray for anymore.

First off, you're not lazy or spiritually apathetic if you're experiencing any of these realities; you're recalibrating. Seasons of change require adjusting and adapting, and sometimes that adaptation is exhausting, which is precisely why we need God's strength through it all.

Here's what I know: If prayer got you here, prayer can get you through. It might take some reevaluating when the old rhythms of prayer don't seem to be working anymore. It might take learning how to bring your own fruit basket of emotions to God without shame. No matter how tired, frazzled, or emotional we feel, it delights God when we come to him. And there is no safer place to let your emotions be in motion than in the presence of God.

JENEE'S BITTERSWEET SEASON

In chapter 3 I told you about my friend Jenee. She and I were both living in seasons of answered prayers in Florida and also were thrust into unpacking past traumas in therapy. Life was a juxtaposition, feeling blessed on the outside and like a mess on the inside as we navigated our Bittersweet Seasons. You could say our seasons fell into Seasons of Balancing too. Like I said in the beginning, sometimes your season will fit into more than one category. But due to the nature of the heavy past traumas we were both unpacking in therapy, Bittersweet feels fitting. We felt grateful to have each other to relate to in our Good Grief!

Jenee is admirable for so many reasons: She's a CrossFit competitor, a supermom of six kids, an avid reader, and a faithful servant. But one of the qualities I admire most about Jenee is her heart for prayer. When I was searching for a snack in Jenee's pantry once, I saw a list on the wall of the prayers she was praying for her kids. It was full of Scriptures and specific ways she was covering them in prayer. Seeing that on her wall made me realize something: Whoever was in Jenee's orbit was getting prayed for, whether they asked for it or not.

Prayer has been foundational for Jenee from the very beginning of her walk with Jesus. All the good things she was celebrating in Florida were a result of persistence in prayer: her husband's promotion, their new house, the kids thriving in their friendships. She could trace the hand of God in this season back to prayers she prayed in the last one. But something was breaking open as Jenee began her work in therapy, and her approach to prayer wasn't working anymore.

Jenee's heart was open and raw; her bouts of crying and panic attacks made her feel exposed and vulnerable. Before she came to know God, the only times she would cry out to him were in times of desperation—times she was a mess. But she was a Christian now. Weren't her prayers supposed to be pretty and polished? Now that she knew God, she could quote Scripture, pray with a systematic process, intercede for others, and engage in prayer with authority. Why would she want to go backward, back to messy and broken? But God was revealing himself to Jenee in a different way. What Jenee saw as a sign of regression, God was showing her was progression; she was progressing in intimacy. It's only those we are closest with who see us at our most vulnerable. God was inviting her to come as she was—unkept, broken, in the messy middle. Being raw before God didn't mean she was in the same mess she was in before; it meant that she was allowing God to become her safe place no matter how strong or weak she felt.

God was teaching Jenee how to be vulnerable with him so she could learn how to be vulnerable with others. He wanted her to drop the facade, be open and broken before him, and allow him into areas where she'd unknowingly built walls.

Jenee and I became SOS prayer partners. We never officially designated this role in each other's lives; it just happened over time. If one of us was slipping into a hard moment or a hard day, all we had to do was pick up the phone and call. Usually our prayer calls took place while I was sitting on my back patio, and every time, Jenee would comment on the birds singing in the background. "Melissa, there are those birds singing again. God is good. If he takes care of those birds, he's going to take care of us too."*

God's invitation for Jenee to "come as you are" became the theme of our friendship too. The truth is, we all need "come as you are" friends. We need to learn to let others in so we can stand in the gap in prayer for each other during life's toughest moments. Whether our battles are internal or external, big or small, a "come as you are" friend will never make us feel like our battles are petty or insignificant.

When we are struggling with an answer to prayer, there's an element of guilt and shame involved. We kick ourselves because we tell ourselves that we shouldn't feel this way. But guilt and shame can't coexist with the love and empathy of a friend. Learning to let "come as you are" people in and not carry your story all by yourself is not a sign of weakness; it's a sign of spiritual maturity.

If your prayer life feels flat, try the "come as you are" method both with God and with one other safe person. Find yourself an SOS prayer partner, someone you can call when you can't find the words to pray for yourself. In the busiest seasons, a phone call (or even words) isn't needed; Jenee and I agreed that if we text each other the prayer emoji, nothing more needs to be said. If that prayer emoji pops up from Jenee on my phone, I immediately say a prayer,

* Luke 12:24.

even if it's a short prayer in my head in the middle of my workday. Jesus said, "Where two or three gather in my name, there am I with them."* God's presence is with you as your partner in prayer, whether it's in texts, whispered prayers, back porch–phone calls, or emoji-sized cries for help.

Like the birds Jenee always notices in the background, prayer is how we stay in rhythm with each other and with God. Birds don't sing because life is perfect; they sing because that's how they stay connected. Some songs are calls for help. Some are songs of praise. But every note reminds the flock, *You're not alone out here.* And friend, neither are you. When your soul forgets the words, let someone else sing for you. When your prayer comes out breathless, call on a "come as you are" friend to help you find the words. We can bring our Good Grief to our good God and a good friend, because prayer was never meant to be about performance; it's about presence.

THE POWER OF A PRAYER WALK

During my season of change, I craved walks around my neighborhood like a pregnant woman craves ice cream. I couldn't explain it, I didn't understand it, but I just needed to walk and walk and walk. So most mornings I would walk around the neighborhood, taking the longest route possible. And in the evenings I would do the same. Sometimes I'd take the dog with me, but most of the time I wanted to walk alone.

Later in my journey my therapist told me about a technique called *eye movement desensitization and reprocessing* (EMDR). He

---

* Matthew 18:20.

explained that this therapeutic method was discovered in 1987 when Francine Shapiro was walking in the park. She was walking around a small lake when she noticed that eye movements while walking appeared to decrease the intensity of unpleasant emotions. She began experimenting by helping war veterans with PTSD and simulating the same eye movements she experienced while walking. The results were astounding. The bilateral stimulation activates both sides of the brain with the shifting eye movement.[1] This stimulation helps you process painful memories, like opening up an old file in your computer, editing it with truth, and filing it away again. My cravings for walking started to make sense.

I've since discovered that three minutes a day of walking will cause blood pressure to decrease, twenty minutes outside improves mood, and ninety minutes outside can reduce the number of depressive thoughts.[2] Walking also helps your brain. Regular walking has been shown to increase the size of the hippocampus, a region linked to memory and learning.[3] Steve Jobs was famous for holding "walking meetings," because he believed walking helped with creativity and clarity. Some of his biggest decisions were made during these walks. It turns out Steve was right; one Stanford study found that people were up to 60 percent more creative when walking than sitting.[4] Sounds in nature, like rustling leaves or singing birds, have been shown to reduce cortisol levels and improve attention, so there's added benefits for those who opt to walk outside rather than on a treadmill.[5]

Comedian Ryan Hamilton joked on *The Tonight Show*, "I think it's going to baffle historians. 'What happened to these people? They just stopped. We're not sure. They kind of slowly coalesced into a gel, and that was it for them. We have evidence that they were actually counting their individual steps one at a time. That's how little they were moving.'"[6]

One health influencer recently joked, "So I invented this thing called walking." After everything else failed to help her manage perimenopause symptoms, she started walking (with and without a weighted vest), and she swore by the results. Maybe we are looking at all the latest and greatest trends when all we need is to go back to the basics.

C. S. Lewis described how a walk with his friend J. R. R. Tolkien around Magdalen College in Oxford deeply challenged and transformed his thinking about God and Christianity. Shortly after, he embraced faith in Christ.[7] Some of the richest Christian theology and literature exist today because of C. S. Lewis, and it all started with a walk.

When we talk about our journey with God, we often refer to it as our walk with God. And maybe it's not completely metaphorical. In Genesis 12:1 God called Abraham to move to "the land I will show you." The Lord didn't give Abraham geographical directions; the journey would require complete trust in God and a really long walk. In response Abraham packed his bags, gathered his family, and set out, awaiting further instructions from God. The first leg of Abraham's journey was safe and watered, along the Euphrates River. The second leg went straight through the desert: no fishing, no predictability, dry. It seems like God wanted to show Abraham that he was near in the river seasons and near in the dry seasons, as long as they were walking together. And maybe that's why it took so long for the Israelites to reach the promised land. Maybe God wanted to teach them about the slow pace of love and that life is about relationship, not about the destination.

In his book *Three Mile an Hour God*, Kosuke Koyama shared how Jesus walked from town to town, meeting people along the way. He lived a life of presence—not speed—attuned to interruptions, to the sick, to children, to the marginalized. His pace was and is intentional. Koyama's point was this: God chooses to move slowly, because love takes time. He said, "Love has its speed. It is a spiritual speed. It is a different kind of speed from the technological speed to which we are accustomed. It goes on in the depth of life, whether we notice or not, at three miles an hour. It is the speed we walk and therefore the speed the love of God walks."[8]

In the book of Luke, two men were debating and discussing the events pertaining to Jesus's death, not realizing that it was he they were talking to. "As they talked and discussed these things with each other, Jesus himself came up and walked along with them."* I wonder how many of us are too caught up in our own inner dialogues and debates (our minds full of the latest headlines) that we don't even notice when God's presence walks beside us to give us his perspective. If we're moving too fast, we may miss wisdom from God, who refuses to be hurried.

I don't think we can have an effective prayer life if we try to hurry through it all the time, which is why I love a good prayer walk. It forces me to slow down, notice the nature around me and thank God for it, and begin praying with the same unhurried cadence in which I walk. In years past I served with a pastor who paced while he prayed, and I couldn't tell you what moved faster, his mouth or his feet. Everything was a big rush (because nothing is more urgent than demanding a move of God). That's not the kind of prayer walking I'm talking about.

Here's how prayer walking started for me. I started to take one thing that was burdening me—even if it was simply my mismatched emotions—and I would bring it to God while I walked.

* Luke 24:15.

My prayers were simple, and my pace wasn't rushed. I would focus on putting one foot in front of the other, and I would say, *God, I don't know how to solve this, but I know you do*, or *God, I feel overwhelmed, but I know you are bigger.* It became my daily act of providing space for my emotions to be in motion with God.

If you loved the science on the benefits of walking, you'll appreciate these benefits of prayer. Dr. David H. Rosmarin, a clinical psychologist and Harvard Medical School professor, explained that prayer can soothe the nervous system, quiet the fight-or-flight response, and reduce emotional reactivity and anger.[9] One study found that participants who engaged in repeating phrases like "God is love" experienced less anxiety and more tolerance to pain than those using secular or nonspecific sayings. Dr. Amy Wachholtz compared the mental effect of prayer to handing off a heavy backpack. "It lets you put down your burden mentally for a bit and rest," she said.[10]

Research shows that structured rhythmic prayers regulate breathing to about six breaths per minute—an optimal pace for cardiovascular health and stress reduction.[11] Prayer activates the parasympathetic nervous system (the "rest and digest" system), which can lower stress hormones, support immune balance, and improve emotional stability.[12] And last but not least, prayer is shown to help with coping and promoting hope and a sense of meaning during hardship.[13] When you partner the benefits of walking with the benefits of prayer, it's a powerful combination. And not to mention what's taking place in the spiritual realm when we invite heaven to earth.

I will never ignore or underestimate the power of a prayer walk again. Whenever I feel the urge, I slip my shoes on and begin walking with God. Because there are files in my brain that need to be reopened and reprocessed, emotions that need to be put in motion, and burdens I try to carry on my own that are too heavy to carry alone. And if I want to experience and emulate the love of God in my life, I have to learn to walk at his pace, not mine.

Maybe you don't feel like this is a slowdown season; maybe you're up to your eyeballs in kids, bills, car lines, or projects at work. I know the feeling deeply, friend. Who has time to slow down, go on a prayer walk, or sit in God's presence when the to-do list is a mile long? I get it. I always thought slowing down was a peaceful act, but what I've learned is that it's also a battle strategy. It's not always an act of peace; sometimes it's an act of war. Sometimes you need to reclaim peace in your life boldly. Sometimes you need to fight for your joy resolutely. Sometimes you need to take back the territory that's been taken from you. I know, it's hard to go to battle when you feel like you need to be in triage. But some seasons require fighting with God's supernatural strength, which is exactly why a prayer walk just might be the thing that saves your life.

The emotions from change fatigue can feel overwhelming and surprising at times. Trust me, I get it. But just like your season of transition is liminal, so are your emotions. Your feelings are not final. And when the emotions feel overwhelming, never underestimate the power of walking with God and surrendering every burden that feels too heavy for your heart to handle. Jesus gave you an invitation to rest when you're weary when he said, "Walk with me and work with me—watch how I do it. Learn the unforced rhythms of grace."* He didn't promise to make all your emotions go away, but did you catch it? He invites you to *walk* with him. He invites you to bring your weary heart and weary emotions to walk in step, and in motion, with him. It's a powerful invitation.

---

* Matthew 11:28–30 MSG.

FIVE MORE MINUTES

Finding new rhythms for a new season takes time. But it's often the smallest tweaks that make the biggest difference. Here are a few examples of the power of small shifts:

- In professional golf one or two strokes per round is the difference between average and the best in the world.
- Only a one-degree difference in temperature makes water go from hot to boiling.
- Eleven Madison Park became the best restaurant in the world by focusing on the "last one inch," the small extra effort to create an unforgettable experience.
- If a pilot adjusts the trajectory of the plane by even the smallest percentage, the plane ends up in an entirely different city.

When it comes to your prayer life, what if you were only one small shift away from finding your new rhythm? What if you only needed to adjust your trajectory by a small amount to land in an entirely different place?

One time, during my whirlwind of change, my pastor gave a challenge to our church. He said, "What if after you thought you were done praying, you prayed for five more minutes?" I'm not sure why this little challenge stuck with me, but I think about it almost every day. And some of my best moments with God have come from that extra five minutes.

When my kids were little, I would read bedtime stories to them. Almost every night they would ask the same question: "Just five more minutes?" They loved spending time with me, hearing my voice, and being near me. Jesus said that to enter the kingdom of heaven, we must turn and become like little children.* God wants us to approach him with childlike anticipation and delight. He wants us to love spending time with him, hearing his voice, and being near him. But when we grow up, our posture shifts from "Just five more minutes?" to "Let's make this quick. I only have five minutes."

It's in those extra five minutes that I often remember to pray for a friend's surgery appointment, a marriage that's struggling, or that person I told, "I'll be praying for you." Or those extra five minutes remind me that I forgot to express gratitude, and I spend the remainder of my prayer time giving thanks. Sometimes those extra five minutes become a way to look at my calendar for the day and invite God into every meeting, conversation, and task ahead.

If you're in a Season of Building, maybe that extra five minutes is a time to remember to slow down and walk with God at a pace that recharges you for your mission. If you're in a Season of Balancing, maybe those five minutes are a time for you to practice honesty before God and to ask him to help you process, balance, and align your emotions. If you're in a Bittersweet Season, maybe those five minutes are a time for you to give your grief and gratitude to a God who understands.

In this chapter I provide a lot of ways you can approach prayer. But the intention isn't to make you feel overwhelmed; you don't have to overhaul your prayer life entirely. The ideas I share are to help you find the small shifts you can make when you are hitting a wall. For me praying honestly, going on prayer walks, and adding five more minutes made a big difference. As you work through the next section, consider how you'll spend your five more minutes. Don't try to do it all; simply pick the approach you need most today.

---

* Matthew 18:3.

Pray It Through

Turning Scripture into prayer provides space for the truth to travel from our heads to our hearts. Here are some verses I've turned into prayers. Pray them out loud and notice which ones resonate with you the most during this season:

God, I trust you, because you are the same yesterday, today, and forever.[*]

God, I will not be afraid of bad news. My heart is firm, trusting in you, Lord.[†]

God, thank you that you will fight for me; I need only to be still.[‡]

God, thank you that my path is like the morning sun, shining ever brighter till the full light of day.[§]

God, thank you that a satisfying and true life is found in your every word.[¶]

God, keep steady my steps according to your promise.[**]

---

* Adapted from Hebrews 13:8.
† Adapted from Psalm 112:6–7.
‡ Adapted from Exodus 14:14.
§ Adapted from Proverbs 4:18.
¶ Adapted from Matthew 4:4.
** Adapted from Psalm 119:133.

Anchor Your Soul

Here are five more ways to put emotion in motion through prayer. Choose one to practice today.

1. PRAY HONESTLY

We can become so accustomed to presenting our polished self to others that we slip into this habit with God. But have you read some of the unfiltered prayers in Scripture? God didn't edit them out of the Bible and include only perfectly polished prayers. He left the humanity in so we can have permission to be human too.

2. JOURNAL TO NAME AND NAVIGATE

Keep a prayer journal to write down what you're feeling, what triggered that feeling, and what truth you want to return to. This is another way to be honest with God but also a way to help you examine and name your emotions. This is similar to Dr. Dan Siegel's therapeutic principle of "name it to tame it" but with the added benefit of inviting God into the process.[14]

Try this prompt: "God, right now I feel . . . , and I think it's because . . . But God, I know you are. . ."

3. WORSHIP

Worship helps give you a higher perspective when you get stuck. When all you can see is how big your problem is, worship reminds you how big God is. And by singing along with the lyrics, worship often gives you words when you don't have your own. Lifting your hands in worship, crying, or singing to God help release emotional energy that might otherwise get stuck.

4. PRAY THROUGH A PSALM

The Psalms are full of emotion; use them as a guide to pray when you're too overwhelmed to find your own words. Reading the Psalms out loud also reminds you that you're not alone in your experience; people (like King David) throughout history have had the same thoughts, feelings, and doubts. Try Psalm 13, 42, 77, or 139.

5. GO ON A PRAYER WALK

Go on a fifteen-minute prayer walk and choose one memory, emotion, or aspect of your life to process while you walk. Pray slow breath prayers that interrupt your thoughts. Here are some you can borrow:

Breathe in: *God, I surrender it to you.*
Breathe out: *God, I receive your strength.*
Breathe in: *God, I believe but help my unbelief.*
Breathe out: *God, fill me with faith.*
Breathe in: *God, I give you my anxiety.*
Breathe out: *God, fill me with your peace.*

Chapter 9

LIVING W.H.O.L.E.: RHYTHMS THAT RESTORE

The key is not to prioritize what's on your schedule but to schedule your priorities.

—STEPHEN R. COVEY

We expect an answer to prayer to feel like opening a present at a birthday party, but—SURPRISE!—it sometimes feels more like the game pin the tail on the donkey. We're blindfolded, a little dizzy, unsure where to place what we've been given, and hoping we don't mess the whole thing up in front of everyone.

When life spins us around, it's easy to lose the rhythms we had in place that made us feel steady to begin with. As for me, I was so consumed trying to balance my new norm, I neglected foundational routines. Maybe you can relate. Before the baby was born, your workout routine was consistent; now it's nonexistent. Before the wedding day, your days off were full of rest and replenishment; now you're lucky to find an hour alone. Before you launched your business, your relationship with God was on fire; now your fire is a flicker.

The answers to our prayers aren't the problem, but our rhythms are. If we want to find our footing, we need to reinvent our routines. They won't look the same as before (which is why it feels like hitting your head against a wall every time you try). Each new season requires a reevaluation of what's working and what's not. We need to examine what's restorative and what's no longer realistic, what to add and what to leave behind.

We need a restorative structure in every season to reorient our bodies, minds, and spirits toward wholeness again. Without the rhythms in place, our brains don't know what to expect or reach for to provide stability and move us forward.

Wayne Muller said, "We can work without stopping, faster and faster, electric lights making artificial days so the whole machine can labor without ceasing. But remember: No living thing lives like this. There are greater rhythms that govern how life grows: seasons and sunsets and great movements of seas and stars. We are a part of the creation story, subject to all its laws and rhythms. To surrender to the rhythms of seasons and flowerings and dormancies is to savor the secret of life itself."[1]

I went running with my Uncle Jim once in the Las Vegas heat. I asked him how he traveled so far every morning, seemingly unfazed by running miles upon miles in the scorching sun. He said, "It's easy. I pick a point in the near distance, and I focus on that point. I don't think about the journey as a whole or how far I need to go.

I just focus on getting to that one point. Then when I reach that point, I pick a new point and start all over again."

My uncle broke up his long morning runs into small milestones. Reaching each milestone gave him a fresh wind.

I can make it to the cactus.

I can make it to the brown house.

I can make it to the mailbox.

I can make it to the fence.

During my season of change fatigue, I noticed something. I was starting to mentally break up time like my uncle does on his runs. I had discovered the power of prayer walking and found my stride with pickleball, and I began to anticipate parts of my day and week as benchmarks and rhythms.

I can make it to church on Sunday.

I can make it to pizza night.

I can make it to pickleball.

I stopped trying to get through the whole season and instead looked for small benchmarks of restoration that kept me moving forward. When I realized how much of a difference it was making, I went back to my calendar and looked for more ways to schedule rhythms—even small ones, like pizza night. The rhythms of rest and replenishment on my agenda kept me tethered on the longest and hardest days of adjustment. If Thursday was dizzying, I knew date night was coming on Friday. If Monday was a blur, I knew I had pickleball that night. If the whole week was hard, I knew church was coming on Sunday.

Mental health practitioners call this the *anticipatory brain*, when your brain begins to anticipate something because it has been trained to prepare for that something.[2] Having daily and weekly rhythms gave my soul stable anchors when life felt unsteady.

In this chapter I'm going to show you how to maximize your anticipatory brain. When you're in a whirlwind of change fatigue, you always need something to look forward to and your soul needs space to breathe. And most important, when you're off balance you need to prioritize your wholeness again. I'm going to show you a new way of being W.H.O.L.E. At the end of each section, I provide a menu of sorts, a list of practical ways you can add new rhythms to your life. When your days seem to blur together and your mind keeps drifting to negative places, it's time to train your brain to stop anticipating doom and gloom and start anticipating breathing room.

WHAT IT MEANS TO BE W.H.O.L.E.

The older I get, the more I've realized that Christ's invitation to follow him is so much different and more beautiful than I ever imagined. Part of that realization was adopting kids who have been through trauma. My goal as their parent was never behavior modification, making sure they acted perfectly or fell in line. My deepest desire for them was wholeness. There was so much robbed from their youth, so much disappointment and loss. What I wanted most was to help them gather up the broken pieces so they could be made whole once again. I'm not a savior or a hero, but wholeness is at the heart of any caring parent with a child who has experienced loss. And I realized that's what God wants for us too. As our Father he wants the brokenness in our lives and hearts restored to wholeness.

Here's a breakdown on why wholeness is God's idea. The word *integrity* stems from the Latin word *integer*, which means "whole and complete." If someone has integrity, they are whole and consistent, meaning there is only one version of that person. (They are not one person behind closed doors and another in public.) In a confusing season of change, you might find yourself saying, "A part of me feels this way, but another part of me feels that way." It's normal for humans to experience these mixed emotions, but sometimes it can lead to mixed behavior (sometimes behavior you aren't proud of because a part of you wants something you know isn't good for you). Parts work is a popular therapeutic technique meant to integrate a divided heart. But God was in the parts-work business long before it was discovered by mental health professionals. One of the names of God is Yahweh-Shalom.* Yahweh is the personal name of God, revealing his eternal, unchanging nature. *Shalom* is a rich Hebrew word that goes far beyond "peace," as we understand it in English. It means "wholeness, completeness, harmony, well-being, and restoration."

So together Yahweh-Shalom means

- "the Lord who makes me whole,"
- "the God who brings peace, even in chaos," and
- "the One who restores and puts all the pieces back together."

God is complete, lacking nothing, fully integrated—"the same yesterday and today and forever."† God doesn't have a divided heart, and he wants to take the parts of us that feel divided and put all the pieces back together again.

In modern Israel when someone greets you or says goodbye, they typically say, "Shalom." They are saying more than hello or

* Judges 6:24 NLT.
† Hebrews 13:8.

goodbye and more than "Peace be with you." They are saying something more along the lines of "May you be filled with a complete and perfect peace and be full of well-being." *Shalom* extends beyond a happy greeting; the word evokes a soul-level state of fullness, soundness, wholeness, and complete reconciliation.

When Jesus said, "Be perfect, therefore, as your heavenly Father is perfect," he was using a Greek word similar to *shalom*—*teleioó*—meaning "complete in all its parts."* Jesus wasn't calling people to the idea of a perfect Sunday best as we might imagine; he was inviting people into a life of God-like wholeness. In other words, be whole and complete, like your heavenly Father, the one who is full of integrity, trustworthy, and without duplicity. Invite all your broken, confusing, and divided parts to meet him at the cross and become whole like him.

So when Jesus said to the fisherman, "Follow me," it meant much more than academic learning.† It meant "come become like me." It wasn't about a life of limitation but a life of imitation. And amid all our disorientation in the shifting seasons of our lives, I believe Jesus still extends this invitation to us today. *Become like me; be whole.*

When Jesus expressed that the greatest commandment is to "love the Lord your God with all your heart," the Greek word for *all* is *holos*, meaning—you guessed it—"whole or complete."‡ Are you sensing a theme here? In fact, *holos* refers to all the parts present and working as a whole. Loving God and others with our whole hearts is difficult if our hearts are divided and our lives are disconnected. But God invites us into a better way, a way where our hearts are

* Matthew 5:48.
† Matthew 9:9.
‡ Matthew 22:37.

reconciled and where the rhythms in our lives care for *all* of us—the *whole* of us—not just one part.

James 1:2–4 says, "My fellow believers, when it seems as though you are facing nothing but difficulties, see it as an invaluable opportunity to experience the greatest joy that you can! For you know that when your faith is tested it stirs up in you the power of endurance. And then as your endurance grows even stronger, it will release perfection into every part of your being until there is *nothing missing and nothing lacking*" (TPT, emphasis mine).

So here's what changed my life and what will change yours: a rhythm of wholeness that prioritizes each domain of life. A way of living that will restore your equilibrium in your physical health, emotional health, mental health, spiritual health, and social life. It's a way of following Jesus that values you as the whole individual God created you to be—nothing divided, nothing missing, nothing lacking.

Here's what W.H.O.L.E. looks like:

Wellness (Physical)
Heart (Emotional)
Outlook (Mindset)
Life with God (Spiritual)
Engagement (Relationships)

WELLNESS: A RHYTHM OF NOURISHMENT FOR YOUR PHYSICAL HEALTH

Do you remember Elijah's Bittersweet Season? Elijah prayed for God to show his power at Mount Carmel, and fire came down from heaven. All the people who witnessed the miracle fell prostrate and cried, "The LORD—he is God! The LORD—he is God!"* It was a victorious moment of ministry, but right after, Elijah was thrown a curveball. He was sent a death threat that made him so fearful and discouraged that he actually asked God to take his life. Here's how God responded:

> Then [Elijah] lay down under the bush and fell asleep.
>
> All at once an angel touched him and said, "Get up and eat." He looked around, and there by his head was some bread baked over hot coals, and a jar of water. He ate and drank and then lay down again.
>
> The angel of the Lord came back a second time and touched him and said, "Get up and eat, for the journey is too much for you." So he got up and ate and drank. Strengthened by that food, he traveled forty days and forty nights until he reached Horeb, the mountain of God. There he went into a cave and spent the night.†

God responded to Elijah's despondence by sending an angel to make sure he had food, water, and rest. God wanted to make sure Elijah was nourished and that his physical body was cared for and prioritized. Taking care of our bodies is not unspiritual; it was God, speaking through the apostle Paul, who called our bodies "temples of the Holy Spirit."‡

For the first two years at my new job, I had a strange shoulder pain. I tried chiropractic care, massage therapy, shockwave therapy, stretching, ointments and creams, lumbar support—you name

---

* 1 Kings 18:16–39.
† 1 Kings 19:5–9.
‡ 1 Corinthians 6:19.

it. I thought it was the stress of change fatigue, but one day my chiropractor asked me how much water I drank. "Not much," I admitted. He told me he thought my muscles needed more hydration and to try drinking more water. After I took his advice, my shoulder pain was gone. Sometimes we wonder why we feel out of sorts, and the answer is that we've forgotten something basic, like drinking water. The angel sent to Elijah didn't say or do anything profound. He had Elijah eat a nourishing meal, hydrate, and rest.

Developing a rhythm of prayer walking, pickleball, eating better meals, and hydrating well helped me find my equilibrium when I was in the depths of my season of change. I noticed that if my morning started off with a good meal, I had the strength and focus to start my routine with my prayer journal on the patio. The act of caring for my body directly impacted my ability to care for my spirit. Therapist and author Deb Fileta said it this way: "We want to attack everything with Bible verses right away without realizing that God made us as holistic beings. And if my brain isn't working right now, I can't even process a Bible verse."[3]

Practical Ways to Prioritize Wellness

Daily Wellness Rhythms

- Create a consistent bedtime and wake-up routine.
- Drink plenty of water with electrolytes.
- Go for a fifteen-minute prayer walk each day.
- Work out or plan for movement or stretching.
- Choose one nourishing meal or smoothie that is a nonnegotiable.

Weekly Wellness Rhythms

- Plan an easy-dinner night (like Friday pizza night or Sunday leftovers).
- Play a sport (like pickleball).
- Have one day of grocery shopping and meal prepping.
- Go on a hike or a longer walk.
- Do a sleep space reset (change sheets, declutter nightstand, reset diffuser).
- Honor the Sabbath.

Monthly Wellness Rhythms

- Book a massage, chiropractor, or other wellness appointment.
- Try a new recipe or a healthy product swap.
- Talk to your doctor about how you're feeling and schedule bloodwork or hormone testing, if needed.

Heart: A Rhythm of Guarding, Processing, and Healing Your Emotions

I used to see emotions like a horse to break or a war to win. I wanted to control, contain, and direct. But now I see the heart like a garden, with our emotions as something to be tended to and cultivated instead of conquered and overpowered.

In her book *The Garden Within*, Dr. Anita Phillips brilliantly explains this concept: "Emotions are consistently cast as the opposition in a war that never seems to end. The scorched earth of your heart bears the scars, but your heart was never meant to be a battlefield. Your heart is a garden."[4] She goes on to say, "You don't need to overthrow your emotions to experience a revolution in your life. You just need to overthrow the lies you have believed about your emotions. The Creator designed your heart to be a garden, not a war zone. A truly powerful life isn't won. It's cultivated."[5]

Hildegard of Bingen, a twelfth-century German Benedictine abbess and theologian, also used the imagery of a garden for our souls and emotions, saying we must "root out the useless grasses, thorns, and briars" in order to reveal the beauty of God's image glistening in the soil.[6] For Hildegard sin was not just wrongdoing; it was neglect. Failing to water and care for the soil meant losing its life-giving "greening power."[7]

Like any garden, our hearts need consistent attention to flourish. Living a life of distraction to avoid our emotions is a recipe for a lot of thornbushes and weeds. I look back and cringe at the number of thornbushes and briars that were growing in the garden of my heart in my twenties. Sure, I had Jesus, and I sat in church every week. But I was full of envy, pain, entitlement, insecurity, and pride. Not because Jesus wasn't doing a work in my life but because I was using spiritual language and tools to bypass my emotions. Peter Scazzero said, "Emotional health and spiritual maturity are inseparable. It is not possible to be spiritually mature while remaining emotionally immature."[8]

Over time I developed a rhythm of going to therapy regularly and participated in an inner healing modality called HeartSync. I learned the value in naming my emotions before God, even when I wasn't proud of them (that very process minimizes their power). My husband and I created a weekly rhythm of sharing what was on our hearts. Sometimes nothing got solved, but we felt more connected simply by talking about our emotions. I also started a small group that ended up feeling like group therapy. I bought a prayer journal that prompts me to name what I'm afraid of each day but also invites me to name who God is over my circumstances. All these rhythms in my life cultivated a much healthier garden in my heart than what I had in my twenties. Now, because I have routines for my emotions built into my life, my heart doesn't feel cluttered, and the good stuff isn't getting choked out by all the weeds.

Proverbs 4:23 says, "Above all else, guard your heart, for everything you do flows from it." The word *guard* seems to get lost in translation. We think it's our job to put up armor, to put our hearts on lockdown, or to deny our emotions. But the word *guard* comes from the Hebrew word *natsar*, which means "to protect, maintain, watch, or keep." So, like faithful gardeners, we need to tend to our emotions with care and consistency.

Practical Ways to Prioritize Your Heart

Daily Heart Rhythms

- Write in a prayer journal and name what you're feeling before God without editing or pretending.
- Listen to calming worship or instrumental music.
- Take a short prayer walk to breathe and let feelings rise and release.
- Practice gratitude or repeat a declaration that aligns your feelings with truth.
- Limit exposure to high-drama environments, doomscrolling, and social media spirals.

Weekly Heart Rhythms

- Spend time with someone you feel emotionally safe with, and be vulnerable.
- Reflect in your journal, *How have I handled my emotions this week? What did I learn?*
- If you're married, set aside time for a heart-to-heart conversation.
- Attend a small group that centers around a topic that promotes emotional health.
- Read or pray through a psalm (especially when you need unfiltered language for your emotions).
- Meet with a therapist (this could also be monthly or bimonthly).
- Spend time in nature.

Monthly Heart Rhythms

- Connect with a mentor, pastor, or therapist.
- Spend extended time journaling your story and reflect on how you've grown.
- Ask God, *How do you want me to tend to my heart this month?* and write down what comes up.
- Schedule a day to rest and recalibrate.

Outlook: A Rhythm of Protecting and Feeding Your Mindset

When I was deep in my feelings of grief and guilt, my mentor, Julie, gave me advice that changed my life. She said, "When you can't change the way you feel, change the way you think." At the time I didn't want to hear it. I knew no amount of positive thinking was going to pull me out of my pit. And while it was true that I needed to unpack some things in therapy and process my feelings, it was also true that there were practical ways I could grow in my mindset, reframe my thoughts, and reclaim my peace.

Sometimes my thoughts lined up with my feelings. But other times my feelings were in the driver's seat, and I needed to remind them that they were welcome on the journey but not at the steering wheel.

Brené Brown once shared a story about how she took her husband to Lake Travis in Texas to go for a swim. When they arrived at the lake, her husband said, "Yeah. Water's good," and swam off. Brené felt embarrassed, feeling like her husband's actions were dismissive. She recognized that she had formed a narrative about what her husband was thinking about her body in a swimsuit. She opened up to him by saying, "The story I'm telling myself is . . ." And it turns out he wasn't thinking anything like that. Brené's story has stuck with me all these years. I've used that phrase to open the door to vulnerability with others but also to open the door for myself.

By saying, "The story I'm telling myself is . . . ," you are automatically opening up the possibility that the story might not be true. You're admitting that you can't believe everything you think.

Our brains can craft compelling stories that shape our lives, and we often step into these stories the longest. So we must hold them with caution and be careful because some are simply fiction and some form our most harmful beliefs. We need to continually commit to renewing our minds with truth.

Give your mind the space it needs to be honest but also the courage it needs to write a new script. Ask yourself, *What is the story I'm telling myself?* And then write down other possible ways to tell that same story.

Here are some examples of stories I realized I was telling myself and how I flipped the script. (I even put notes in my phone of better stories I could come back to when I felt stuck in my thoughts.)

The story I was telling myself: *I don't have what it takes to succeed at my new job.*

Flipping the script: *What if I sharpen my skills, learn, and grow beyond what I thought possible? What if God has me at this job for a reason?*

The story I was telling myself: *I don't have what it takes to help my kids heal.*

Flipping the script: *What if I get a front-row seat to God's miracles in their lives?*

The story I was telling myself: *I'll feel displaced in Florida forever.*

Flipping the script: *What if this is just one chapter in a much bigger story God is writing? What if home isn't as far away as it seems?*

Here's the truth: If your mind is going to gravitate toward worst-case what-ifs, you're going to have to intentionally train it to ask better questions and tell better stories. We don't know the future—we aren't God—but we can open ourselves up to possibilities other than doom and gloom.

Practical Ways to Prioritize Your Outlook

Daily Outlook Rhythms

- Write down your to-do list or any mental clutter to clear your mind.
- Keep a note in your phone that reminds you of better stories when you're stuck.
- Read three to ten pages of a devotional or book that helps you grow your mindset.
- Read Scripture and meditate on what you've read throughout the day.
- Pray and ask God to help you have his higher perspective.

Weekly Outlook Rhythms

- Do something creative that gives your brain a break (like painting, baking, journaling, or rearranging a room).
- Clean out one area of your home or workspace that feels mentally draining.
- Pick a day (like the Sabbath) to turn off notifications on your phone or switch to grayscale mode.
- Write down your anxious thoughts, then reframe them with truth (include a verse or declaration).

Monthly Outlook Rhythms

- Learn something new (like an instrument, language, or hobby).

- Spend time with someone who has a mindset that you admire.
- Visit an art gallery or a creative space or go to a concert for inspiration.
- Examine the impact social media or the news has on you and reevaluate your limits.
- Watch a documentary about a story of triumph.

Life with God: A Rhythm of Prioritizing Your Connection with Your Creator

Have you ever done an obstacle ropes course where you had to let go of one rope before grabbing the next? The feeling of being untethered is frightening, and it's exactly how it feels during times of major transition. When we haven't found solid ground yet, our brains are looking for ways to be tethered and grab the next rope. The beauty of our relationship with God is that he is the steady anchor we can always grab hold of—no matter what season we are in. But just like any relationship, our connection with God requires intentionality and consistency. When we prioritize our time with God as a nonnegotiable on our calendars, we are giving our anticipatory brain a connection point to look forward to, the next rope to grab hold of that truly becomes a lifeline.

John Mark Comer said this about a weekly rhythm with God (or the Sabbath): "The Hebrew word *Shabbat* means 'to stop.' But it can also be translated 'to delight.' It has this dual idea of stopping and also of joying in God and our lives in his world. The Sabbath is an entire day set aside to follow God's example, to stop and delight."[9]

Exodus 20:8 tells us to "remember the Sabbath day, to keep it holy" (ESV). In other words, don't just keep the Sabbath; remember it. Don't just take a day of rest; remember that day of rest is coming. We need our anticipatory brain to expect it, plan for it, prioritize it, and most important, look forward to it.

Another hard day might be coming. Another day of trying to find your footing, feeling out of sorts, and trying to adapt to change. But guess what is also coming if you prioritize it? A moment with God, a day of rest, a prayer walk, or a church service. One moment in God's presence can change everything, but you need to make room. The more distracted and busy you are, the less likely you are to hear him speak through all the noise.

Practical Ways to Prioritize Your Life with God

Daily Life with God Rhythms

- Sit in silence and solitude with God.
- Practice breath prayers (see the end of chapter 8 for examples).
- Start your day with five minutes of prayer, five minutes of worship, and five minutes of Scripture reading.
- Write in a prayer journal.

Weekly Life with God Rhythms

- Use your Sabbath in ways that help you feel connected to God and rested.
- Go on a prayer walk.

- Journal your prayers and gratitude.
- Attend church.
- Be a part of a small group, Bible study, or weekly class.

Monthly Life with God Rhythms

- Read a faith-based book that inspires and deepens your understanding of God.
- Fast from something to create more space for clarity, prayer, or vision.
- Review past entries of your prayer journal to reflect on God's faithfulness.

Engagement: A Rhythm for Your Relationships

When seasons change, often so do our relationships. I still remember after I had my firstborn having to say no to my usual impromptu coffee dates with friends because I didn't want to interrupt my daughter's nap time. It's tempting to cling to the way our relationships and friendships used to operate, but that's not life. It's hard to reevaluate our friendships and find ways to dive deeper with the right people, especially when life is busier than ever. Although seeking friendships takes more energy and effort than we probably feel like we have to give, the reward is more than worth it.

As for me and my season of change, I started a small group. I hand-selected ladies I wanted to get to know more. In the first couple of rounds of our group, I was discouraged. The conversation was good, but I was craving something deeper. My soul needed a safe space to admit how much I was struggling. There comes a pivotal moment in friendship when you have to decide to release your grip or give it more time. I'm so glad I gave it more time. It turns out they were the right group of women, but the format for our group needed adjusting. When one group member introduced a book about anxiety and depression, we all agreed to give it a chance. What I wasn't expecting was for that book to springboard our conversations into the deep end every single week. I had the right ladies, the right time in the week, and even the right location—but what we really needed was a better springboard for discussion.

To this day those ladies and I have a group text thread where we share prayer requests; we have a rhythm of getting together every time I come into town and a virtual book study we continue throughout the year. There's nothing I wouldn't share with that group. Sometimes a little more time and a small tweak make all the difference. I have deep, rich, vulnerable, "talk and pray about the hard stuff" friendships now (that are also superfun), but they took a long time to cultivate. Now that I know the difference, I'd rather be lonely than have shallow friendships.

In his research on blue zones (places with the longest-living people on the planet), Dan Buettner shared that knowing you have at least three to five people to lean on is a powerful antidote to stress, depression, and chronic illness. In Okinawa, Japan, people form *moais*, tight-knit social groups of four to five friends who commit to supporting each other for life. These *moais* share everything from meals to money to encouragement. Members of a *moai* check on each other daily, and this deep relational safety net is considered crucial to their emotional resilience and physical health and is one of their secrets to longevity.[10]

In one research study, participants were asked to estimate the steepness of a hill either alone or accompanied by a friend. Those who were standing next to a friend consistently rated the hill as less steep than those who were alone.[11] The steepness of the hill didn't change, but the perception did. Even if your circumstances stay the same, by not facing them alone, you gain a perspective that makes whatever hill you're climbing in life easier to face.

Practical Ways to Prioritize Engagement

Daily Engagement Rhythms

- Greet your loved ones warmly with eye contact and a smile.
- Pray for one person by name each morning.
- Voice memo a friend instead of texting (low pressure, high connection).
- Get curious in a conversation and ask questions.
- Notice and name one way someone made your day easier or brighter.
- Eat at least one meal with someone else, even if it's just sitting together without screens.
- Listen intently in a conversation (no multitasking or looking at your phone).
- Share a funny video or meme with someone.

Weekly Engagement Rhythms

- Spend time with someone who gets you but who also helps you become your best.
- Initiate a dinner, coffee connect, or fun outing (this

might be monthly, depending on your season).

- Go first in vulnerability with someone you trust.
- Connect in a small group and aim to get to know one person deeper.
- Send a "thinking of you" text to someone you haven't talked to in a while.
- Compliment someone or send them an encouraging Bible verse.

Monthly Engagement Rhythms

- Look at your calendar and cancel or adjust social obligations that aren't life-giving or in alignment with this season.
- Plan something fun with friends (like attending a comedy show, having a game night, or taking a walk together).
- Celebrate something—no matter how small—with people you love.
- Evaluate your relational capacity and ask God to show you who to invest in during this season.
- Serve or encourage someone else (write a note, drop off a treat, offer support).

Pray It Through

God, I want to be whole as you are whole. I pray that you would help me set rhythms in my life that would keep me anchored and steady through my season of change. Give me wisdom to assess what you have for me in this season and the strength to let go of what is no longer serving a purpose in my life. Restore any areas of brokenness and integrate any divided parts of my heart through these life-giving rhythms. Amen.

Anchor Your Soul

Highlight or circle any of the rhythms in each category that feel authentic to you. Put one from each domain on your calendar (in dizzying seasons, it's easy to forget if you don't have a reminder). Make them nonnegotiable. If that feels too permanent, don't worry; you can always change it later or try something new. Reassess each week or month if a rhythm worked for you or if something needs adjusting. Don't give up if your new rhythms don't work the first week or the first month. Keep tweaking your daily, weekly, and monthly rhythms until you find the best fit for you and your family (and reevaluate in each new season). Like the ocean tides, you'll find the highs and lows, the times to give out and the times to take in, peak times and times of rest. The most rewarding part of your new rhythms won't be that you accomplished more but rather that you gave yourself what you needed to show up as your *whole* self.

Chapter 10

MAKING SELF-COMPASSION YOUR SUPERPOWER

The work of paying compassionate attention is, in a sense, learning to steward for ourselves what God already believes about us—that we're valuable and loved.

—AUNDI KOLBER

I have a confession: I've developed some superpowers. I know, I hate to brag or overshadow your favorite Marvel hero, but it's the truth.

Here are a few superpowers I gained during my years of change fatigue.

1. I can cook dinner, answer a homework question, referee a sibling argument, understand a text from my teen that says, "bro idk tbh it's mid but im lowkey not okay," and hide in the bathroom all at the same time.
2. I can remain completely unfazed when a lizard, frog, bug, or bat falls out of my patio umbrella. I've seen things. I've adapted.
3. I can quickly switch from a load of laundry to a Zoom meeting and mute myself just in time to yell, "Get your shoes on!" without anyone knowing.
4. And in all seriousness, I can now interrupt my inner critic without skipping a beat and give myself grace when I need it most.

I've come a long way from the survival mode I was in at the beginning of my journey. I remember the days when thoughts of how I *should* feel and what I *should* have done consumed me. One therapist stopped me and said, "Stop *should*-ing all over yourself." Oof.

Over the years I learned how to accept God's grace and give myself grace too. I learned how to stop beating myself up for unexpected emotions and start welcoming them with curiosity. I learned how to stop looking back with regret and start looking forward with strength. And I learned how to give myself permission to be human, bad days and all.

Now my new spidey senses include being able to spot when someone else is being hard on themselves. It pains me because I know what it's like to circle the drain with guilt, shame, and the feeling that I'm the only one to blame. I love being a safe and gentle sounding board for people who are in process, because empathy eradicates shame, and I will happily join God in the business of shame killing.

So if you're stuck should-ing all over yourself like I was, I hope this chapter provides a soft place for you to land. I hope to provide you with the practical and spiritual tools that will help you come up for air, give yourself grace, and shift your inner critic to inner compassion.

DON'T TALK ABOUT GOD'S DAUGHTER THAT WAY

When I was a young newlywed, I struggled with many insecurities. One day I made a critical comment about myself, and my new husband stopped me in my tracks. He smiled and said, "Don't talk about my wife that way."

Until then, no one had interrupted my negative self-talk that poignantly. My self-criticism spilled out everywhere but remained unchallenged. But now I was someone's wife, and he wasn't going to allow anyone to speak negatively about me—not even me!

In the thick of my season of should-ing all over myself, my husband's little phrase became a tool I learned to twist and use for myself. When self-condemning thoughts popped up, I began to interrupt them.

I should feel differently than this, what is wrong with me? I'm such a failure.

"Don't talk about God's daughter that way."

I should have responded differently. I'm never going to get it right.

"Don't talk about God's daughter that way."

I should be better than this. I should be further along by now.

"Don't talk about God's daughter that way."

We often think and say things about ourselves that we wouldn't speak or think about a coworker, an acquaintance, a friend, or even a stranger. The harsh reality is that the devil doesn't need to come knocking at our doors because we are proficient at doing his job for him. We become our own adversaries, our own accusers, our own worst critics. Sure, maybe some whispers are from the Enemy, but how often do we take the ball he threw and run it right into the end zone? When we leave those thoughts uninterrupted, we let lies linger (or worse, we feed them), forming narratives about our identity that we were never meant to absorb. We need to learn how to align ourselves with a voice that advocates on our behalf. Listen to Jesus's words about the role of the Holy Spirit in our lives: "But the Helper (Comforter, Advocate, Intercessor—Counselor, Strengthener, Standby), the Holy Spirit, whom the Father will send in My name [in My place, to represent Me and act on My behalf], He will teach you all things. And He will help you remember everything I have told you."*

Your Advocate is with you and he is for you and he promises to bring to your remembrance the truth of what he's told you. When self-condemning thoughts start to creep in, will you listen to the accusations or will you listen to the Advocate? Can you take what the Holy Spirit brings to your remembrance and learn to advocate for yourself? Do you have the courage to interrupt your thoughts with the same protectiveness that a father has over his daughter? Because some of the thoughts and words you've left unattended are things your Father in heaven would never think or say about his child.

---

* John 14:26 AMP.

Imagine standing on the playground talking to a young child the way you talk (or think) about yourself. Now imagine the child's loving father is standing right there, listening to it all.

You're a failure.

You can't ever get it right.

You should be further along by now.

You can't ever do anything right.

Look, you messed up again! Figures.

You shouldn't feel that way. There's something wrong with you.

You're broken.

You should be ashamed of yourself.

Can you imagine how infuriated that father would feel watching you speak so harshly to his child? Yet we speak and think these things about God's daughters—ourselves—all the time. What if we took the position of the loving father rather than the accuser? What if we aligned ourselves with a voice of protection rather than a voice of rejection?

As I'm raising teen girls, I've never been more thankful for the precedent that was set all those years ago. My girls and I hold each other accountable for how we talk about ourselves. If one of us slips up, we playfully say, "Don't talk about my sister/mom/daughter that way!"

It doesn't mean we pretend we're the latest and greatest. But I want to teach my girls that there's a way we can be honest about our weaknesses, mistakes, or areas for growth (and even laugh about them) that doesn't undermine our God-given strengths, identity, or potential to grow.

If left unchecked, our self-condemning thought process might look something like this:

1. **We have a feeling and draw a conclusion.** We experience an emotion like guilt, shame, or self-condemnation and conclude something negative about ourselves (like *I'm a failure*).
2. **We gather evidence to support our conclusion.** This sounds something like, *It makes sense that I'm a failure, because I overreacted with my child the other day, I can't seem to keep up with the housework, and I've gained more weight since last year.*
3. **We confuse the evidence for the cause.** We forget that the emotion came first and the proof was gathered later. Before we know it we're knee-deep in a story we never meant to write. *I am a failure, and I know I'm a failure because all the evidence adds up. And because I'm a failure, I'm unworthy of good things.*

Instead of taking time to compassionately tend to our emotions, we jump to conclusions. It's faster that way. We've got reasons to back up our conclusions. The neuropathways are well ingrained and well traveled; it's a quick and easy route back to "I'm a failure." And after we gather enough evidence against ourselves, it's pretty easy to add the next mistake to the list. But it's not the truth (as hard as it pretends to be); it's self-condemnation disguised as logic. Conviction is from the Holy Spirit, who helps us identify the disordered desires (or sin) in our hearts. Conviction leads to a place of repentance, hope, and a closer connection with God. Condemnation is a dead-end road. It attacks our identity, doesn't bring hope, and drives us away from God in shame. Do you see the difference?

Maybe you're in a Season of Building, and you beat yourself up for not having more energy. No matter how hard you try, it seems like there's never enough of you to go around. You jump to the conclusion that it's all your fault and that you're not enough. If only you were better, smarter, stronger, or more like *them* (whoever your "them" is). When you're trapped in condemnation, you can't see the bigger picture that God is omnipresent and you are not, that this is a temporary season, and that relying on God's grace doesn't make you weak; it makes you strong. You are unable to give yourself grace as you adjust, so you slam the gavel and pronounce your failure.

Maybe you're in a Bittersweet Season, and you can't help but think that you should be stronger or that you should be over it by now. Instead of giving yourself room to carry both grief and gratitude, you shame yourself for not being able to pull yourself together and smile through the pain. You get tired of the mental battle and conclude that you're weak, you're not as faith-filled or as strong as others, and you're just too much.

Or maybe your Season of Balancing has left you wrapped in guilt for your mismatched feelings, and you keep asking yourself the dead-end question, *What's wrong with me?* Instead of compassionately responding to yourself and receiving God's grace, you end up with the conclusion that you are broken beyond repair.

We can learn a thing or two from how eagles handle getting pestered. Crows are the only birds that dare to peck eagles, but an eagle doesn't waste time fighting back or even try to shake off the crow. It simply flies higher. As the eagle climbs, the air thins, and the crow is unable to breathe at that higher altitude. It eventually falls away. The same is true for your inner critic. You don't need to keep confusing feelings with facts and collecting evidence against yourself. All you're doing is giving the crow of criticism more access.

You need to rise higher so the critical voice loses oxygen. Condemnation can't survive in an atmosphere of compassion.

Stop wasting your strength intermingling with the crow and fly at a higher altitude. In time what was clinging to you will fall away, not because you fought harder but because you flew higher.

Here's what it looks like to fly higher than your inner critic:

1. **Acknowledge, don't agree.** You can acknowledge that the feeling is real. It's a real cue, a real emotion, a real indicator, a real sensation coming up in your body. But just because the feeling is real doesn't mean it's a fact.

   Catch the thought or feeling in real time and name it: *I think what I'm feeling right now is* __________________ (anxiety, guilt, shame, fear, anger, etc.).

   Then catch the conclusion you came to or were about to come to: *Because of that emotion, it made me think I'm* ______________________ (a failure, behind, broken, etc.).
2. **Shift from accusation to advocacy.** Try asking yourself, *Would my Father in heaven say this about me?* Or *Would I say this about a close friend? What would I tell them instead?*

   Or you can steal my line and say, "Don't talk about God's daughter that way."

   Every child makes bids for their parents' affirmation and reassurance at times. It's okay to ask your Father to reaffirm your identity and value and remind you of the truth. Bring the thought before the Holy Spirit, your Comforter, Counselor, and Defender.

   Ask, *God, what do you say about me?*

   Or pray, *Father, please remind me of the truth of my identity and worth.*

   You might not have time in the moment, but find time

to research and memorize Scriptures about your identity in Christ so the truth is more easily accessible next time. Also, if your critical conclusions feel too concrete, you may decide to seek the help of a therapist who can help you get to the root of past trauma or uncover where the deeply ingrained belief is coming from.

3. **Climb higher.** Like the eagle climbing higher, give the thought less oxygen and focus on more life-giving evidence. Remember, you find what you're looking for. What if instead of looking for reasons that you're a failure, you looked for evidence that you're growing? Or evidence that you're loved? Or evidence of God's faithfulness? This is your opportunity to climb higher in your thoughts. Remember, condemnation can't survive in an atmosphere of compassion. Instead, what if you looked for different evidence? Here are some prompts to get you started:

WHEN YOU FEEL LIKE A FAILURE

- What's one way I showed up, even if it wasn't perfect?
- What would I say to a friend who felt this way?
- In what ways have I grown in this season (no matter how small)?

WHEN YOU FEEL DISORIENTED

- If Jesus were right in front of me, what would he say?
- What are some decisions I've made that I'm proud of?
- What truth do I need to remember right now?

WHEN YOU FEEL STUCK

- What's something I've handled better this month than I would have last year?
- What growth have I seen in myself, even if it's slow or quiet?
- What small win have I overlooked?

This process doesn't mean we bypass our emotions or pretend our feelings aren't real. It means we refuse to let condemnation narrate our stories. We can learn to recognize and name our emotions and thoughts honestly and also decide which ones we allow along for the ride. There's a difference between feeling something and agreeing with it. You can recognize the pesky crow of condemnation is real, and you can choose to lessen its power as you rise toward God's truth. Isaiah 40:31 says, "Those who hope in the LORD will renew their strength. They will soar on wings like eagles; they will run and not grow weary, they will walk and not be faint."

So if the voice of condemnation has been pestering you today, let me call you higher. Don't talk about God's daughter that way.

NO COMPARISONS ALLOWED

In chapter 8 I told you about my SOS prayer partner, Jenee. Jenee called me one day when she needed prayer, and she knew that (at the time) I was in crisis mode with one of my kids. She said, "I know you have bigger problems right now, so I feel bad even asking." But the truth was, Jenee's call was a welcome relief. Jenee calling me, even when I was in the thick of something hard, meant that I had permission to call her when I needed prayer (and it was a time when I needed a lot of prayer!). Like the friend who invites you over when their house is a mess, you have permission to say, "Come on over," when your own house isn't tidy. Her call wasn't an inconvenience; it was an invitation. I told Jenee to never hesitate to call when she needs prayer and to never compare the size of our struggles. If we're struggling, we're struggling, and the beauty of life-giving community is that there's no measuring stick. We get to carry the weight of burdens together, no matter how heavy or light.

It doesn't matter if you're one inch or one mile underwater. If you can't find your way to the surface, you're drowning. So why do we feel like we have to be a mile underwater before we reach out and ask for prayer? Or a mile underwater before we will give ourselves grace? Instead, we tally up the worldwide atrocities, take inventory of the other people who are going through so much more, and decide who *really* needs help (while counting ourselves out). We might be only an inch deep, but we're still drowning.

Sometimes, instead of comparing how small our struggles are to someone else's, we see how smoothly someone else is handling their answer to prayer compared to our own responses. Someone else had an easy pregnancy, and you were on bed rest. Someone else's first year of marriage was bliss, and you haven't been able to go two days in a row without arguing with your husband. Someone else's business or ministry exploded right out of the gate, and you're still grinding. Someone else is handling the teenage years joyfully and without flinching, and you're still crying over baby pictures (guilty!). Whether someone else got handed an easier load or they just seemed to carry the load with ease, things aren't made better when we compare our capacity and circumstances to theirs. We either feel like a weakling or wonder why God dealt us a heavier hand.

The truth is, we don't see the full picture of someone else's story; we just see how they carry it in public or on social media. We all have different capacities, timelines, and terrain to walk. Some of us are climbing steeper hills. Some of us are healing while climbing. And some of us are still feeling confused, carrying our answers to prayer like clunky backpacks.

God isn't grading you on how smoothly you carry your blessing or handing out medals for effortless-looking faith. He's after something deeper: intimacy, honesty, and dependence on him in the process. You don't have to carry it like *she* does. You just have to carry it with him.

The other way we compare ourselves is to past versions of ourselves. I told my sister one day about how I compare myself to the mom I was years ago. Before I adopted and moved to Florida, I was a stay-at-home mom. I homeschooled my three kids. We enjoyed slow mornings, field trips with friends, and Friday Surfdays, and my homemade-meal game was on point. I had more energy and more time, and I never lacked creative ways to connect with my kids.

Now I have five kids instead of three. They are all in different schools, and I work full-time. My mornings aren't nearly as slow, homemade meals are sporadic, and sometimes I feel bad that my youngest isn't getting the same mom that my oldest did. That thought makes me want to cry and hide under my covers.

Maybe you can relate?

You compare the size you are now to the size you were ten years ago.

You compare your energy now to the energy you used to have.

You compare the way you were when you had more time, more finances, or less stress.

You compare the parent you are now to the parent you were when you had fewer kids.

Here's what my sister said to me that shifted my perspective: "Your youngest might not have the same mom, but he gets to see a mom who is working hard to provide for her family. He gets to see a mom who is showing up and persevering even when things are tough. Don't underestimate that." (Who is cutting onions over here?)

Sometimes we don't give ourselves enough grace for being in a different season with a different capacity. We tell ourselves a story that is true, but it's only one way to look at it. And sometimes we need an outsider (like my sister was for me) to help us tell our stories in a different way.

Everything I said is true. I have less time and less creative energy, and there are fewer homemade meals on the table.

But what my sister said is also true. I'm really freaking hard-working, and my kids get a front-row seat to me loving them in a different way.

So if you're comparing yourself to a version of yourself from the past, I hope to be that friend for you today who helps you tell your story in a different way. You are doing your best in a new season with a new capacity. You are still showing up. And if you had only 40 percent to give today and you gave it, you still gave 100 percent (even if your definition of 100 percent looks different than it did a few years ago).

There's a parable in the Bible about a woman who gave only two coins to the temple treasury. Even though many rich people were giving large amounts, Jesus praised the woman who gave her two coins, and he told his disciples that she'd given more than all the others. Why? Because that was her 100 percent. It was all she had. It didn't matter how it measured up to someone else's 100 percent; she gave her all, and God honored it.*

Let's not compare our 100 percent to someone else's, and let's not compare our 100 percent capacity today to what it was yesterday or before we stepped into our answered prayers. God's grace is sufficient for every season, and the moments when we feel weakest are usually when he's shining the brightest. So if you're comparing your capacity to someone else's or to a past version of yourself, take a breath and remember, God doesn't love you for how strong you look or how much you can carry; he loves you because you're his.

PERMISSION TO BE HUMAN

"I know we have a lot of happy, clappy Americans in the room, but I'm afraid we're all being too nice. It's time to be honest," one European man said at my work function in London.

I wasn't sure what he meant by that. But as the days went on, I picked up on more subtleties.

"My blow dryer broke this morning, and my hair looks like garbage," one London local said.

"But your hair is fabulous! You look great!" an American woman piped in.

"Stop. Just don't." The London woman held her hand up. "I know my hair looks like crap, and I don't need you to gloss it over."

Through several more comments and conversations, I

* Mark 12:41–44.

observed how our reputation as Americans was friendly, cheerful, and also annoyingly optimistic to the point of being, dare I say, fake and dismissive. I have one friend from England who once told me, "Americans sound like motivational speakers," and I never understood what she meant by that until my trip to London.

Because there were so many cultures represented in one room (and we all had to work closely with one another), I was able to see my culture contrasted with other cultures in a profoundly perspective-altering way. Although I'm still proud of being a friendly American, I recognize that our strength can also be a weakness if left unchecked. Our incessant positivity can also create a culture that (1) doesn't allow people permission to be human with the full spectrum of human emotions, (2) doesn't leave room for honest feedback . . . and I mean not just the positive kind, and (3) doesn't allow much room for being in-process and embracing the messy middle. One American in the room admitted that growing up she was expected to be a Southern belle: always smiling, always positive, and always put together. Working collaboratively in an environment that expected direct and honest feedback (not just encouragement) was difficult for people who preferred smiles and compliments.

The toxic side to this culture is that we end up unable to give ourselves grace when we need it most. What happens when we experience unexpected or unpleasant emotions? When honesty is hard to swallow? When everyone thinks we are put together, but we're really falling apart?

My American colors showed in my first therapy session when my counselor asked me what I wanted to achieve out of therapy.

With naive confidence I said, "I want to be unshakable. I want to be so strong that nothing affects me."

He smiled and paused for a while before speaking. Then he told me something I didn't want to hear. He said, "Melissa, you will grow and make progress, but you will never be bulletproof, because you are human. The goal of therapy is not to be unemotional and unfazed by everything but to better manage your emotions when they do come."

Dang it. I really liked the bulletproof idea better.

All these years later, his words have stuck with me. Because hard times come, life shifts, emotions are normal, and people who are unfazed by everything are usually jerks.

Having emotions and mindsets to manage doesn't make you weak, and it doesn't mean you aren't depending on God enough. I fear that when it comes to our emotional and mental goals, we are no different from Adam and Eve, who wanted to be like God, in the garden. Only our view of him is skewed. We think that because God is unshakable, he's unemotional. But throughout the gospels Jesus expressed emotions—not just the happy, clappy, culturally acceptable American ones. Jesus wept and grieved; he groaned in anguish and was deeply distressed. He got angry, and he was troubled in spirit. And yet we expect to be emotionally bulletproof?

The word *compassion* comes from the Latin *compati*: *com*, meaning "with," and *passion*, meaning "suffering." The Bible tells us, "You, Lord, are a compassionate and gracious God, slow to anger, abounding in love and faithfulness."* Compassion is a part of God's character and nature. When we need compassion and

---

* Psalm 86:15.

grace, God doesn't observe from a distance; he draws near and enters our world. Jesus is called Immanuel, which means "God with us."* He's with us not just in the celebrations that come with our answers to prayer but also in the sorrow, doubt, mixed emotions, and fear that sometimes follow. He's with us during the confusing times when we don't even understand ourselves. Theologians call this his *co-suffering love*, because it's a love that moves toward pain, not away from it.

If the God of the universe draws near to us in our darkest and most dizzying moments, why would we shame ourselves for simply being human and having human experiences? Self-compassion, then, isn't self-esteem or positive thinking; it's aligning with the heart of God. It's choosing not to reject the parts of ourselves that we wish didn't exist but to invite them to sit with us at the foot of the cross. And when we meet our pain and humanity this way, we create space for healing, not hiding.

The research I included in this book was to help you see that your body, brain, and emotions are responding the way they were designed by your Creator to respond. The problem is when you view your unwanted thoughts and feelings as limiting labels rather than curious clues. Thoughts and feelings are information, not characterization.

A thought or a feeling doesn't define you. It doesn't describe you. And it doesn't characterize you. That's God's job. He says you are his child, chosen and loved. An unexpected thought or feeling is simply information. It's information about something that is happening in your body. Information about something you might

* Matthew 1:23.

need to take to God. Information to take captive so you can renew your mind with truth.

When you face tough emotions or thoughts, give yourself permission to be human. Keep growing and learning, but don't beat yourself up when you have a bad moment or a bad day. Healing is a journey, and the goal is to be better, not bulletproof.

Pray It Through

God, thank you that you are my Advocate. When my thoughts spiral in self-doubt and condemnation, help me to interrupt them with your truth. Help me to respond to myself with grace and compassion. I thank you for the full range of emotions, not just the ones I prefer. Help me to see them as information, not characterization, and to allow my identity to be formed by you, not by my inner critic. Amen.

Anchor Your Soul

Who is the wisest and most compassionate person you know? Keep that friend in mind.

Now that you've given yourself permission to be honest about how you're really feeling, I want you to respond to yourself like your wise and compassionate friend would.

What would they say to you? What advice would they give? What simple reminders of truth would they share? Write down what comes to mind.

Here are some gentler reflection questions to help you look back on your progress and learn to give yourself grace:

1. In what ways have I made my thoughts characterization rather than information?
2. What might my unexpected emotions and thoughts be trying to tell me?
3. What would I say to a good friend who was feeling this way?
4. What is one way I've grown since the beginning of my journey of change?
5. How can I give myself permission to be human (and be in process) today?

CONCLUSION

After spending five years in Florida, I felt anxiety tighten in my chest as we prepared for our next move to Tennessee. *Would this move bring another bout of disorienting change fatigue? Would I go through the same feelings of displacement? Would I feel the same thoughts of regret that I did when I moved to Florida?*

As I shared my fears with my friend Michelle, she said, "Melissa, all the strength and wisdom you've gained in your years in Florida . . . you're taking all of that with you." She was right. Moving is hard, but this time I was taking all my growth along with me in the U-Haul truck.

I braced myself for another dizzying Season of Balancing but hoped maybe I'd move through it faster this time. Only, to my surprise, the mismatched and disorienting feelings didn't follow. Maybe it's because my sister lives ten minutes down the road, or maybe it's the four beautiful seasons or the fireflies glowing amid summer nights. Maybe it's the church on the corner or watching the cousins play together. Maybe it's the way Tennessee reminds me so much of some of the best parts of where I grew up in Oregon. Whatever the reason, moving to Tennessee felt like slipping on a favorite pair of old jeans that fit just right. There was no shock to the system or mismatched emotions. I faced other challenges, but feeling displaced wasn't one of them. Maybe Tennessee is our permanent landing spot, or maybe I already learned what I need to learn and simply don't need to go around the mountain of displacement again (whew!).

We go back and forth to Florida to visit often. We gained forever friends there, a special church community, and a place to vacation with oceans so bright turquoise that it still takes my breath away.

According to an article in *Psychology Today*, out of all life's changes, moving turns out to be the most memorable.[1] A relocation becomes an event people look back on as having major significance in their lives. The University of New Hampshire's Karalyn Enz and colleagues call it the "relocation bump."[2] The distinctive memory of a big move stays with people throughout their entire lives, and I can see why.

It's easy to hear the word *bump* and think of it positively. We want a bump in our salary, a bump in our standard of living, a bump in the weather, or even a baby bump. But some moves feel more like a relocation *slump* than a bump. Memories linked with strong emotions often get seared in the brain, and relocating undoubtedly produces strong emotions. Upon leaving the familiar, the stress of moving, the excitement of something new, the loss of connections, and the start of new ones can surface a mixture of emotions, even when you know it was the right decision.

Until our move to Florida, I had always skimmed over Jesus's response to a scribe who wanted to follow him: "Foxes have holes, and birds of the air have nests, but the Son of Man has nowhere to lay his head."* While I was in Florida, I looked at Jesus's words in light of what it means to carry expectations about *home*. I was talking to a friend on the phone who is relocating to Oregon. She

* Matthew 8:20 ESV.

said, "It really doesn't feel like home here in California anymore, but Oregon doesn't feel like home either. Sometimes I wonder if we aren't meant to feel fully at home because our souls were made for heaven."

Maybe Jesus wanted to give the scribe realistic expectations, because he knew a truth we often forget: Heaven is our home, and it's earth we're passing through. Maybe the reason we feel so unsettled and disillusioned (even after we get what we prayed for) is because we expected something on earth that we will find only in heaven. Our true home rests in another place: eternity. Although we may have preferences—the beach or the mountains, four seasons or year-round warmth—the truth is, we can't expect a place, or an answer to prayer, to fill our souls. Whether it's a move, a new baby, or a different life change that we expected to find comfort in, we must remember that we are citizens of heaven, sojourners on earth.* We are pilgrims passing through a foreign land.† We weren't meant to feel completely settled here. Mixed emotions and restlessness are all a part of what it means to be humans passing through this world, a reminder to turn to God as our source, the only one who truly satisfies.

Throughout the Old Testament, people journeyed to find their dwelling place too. "And they settled there" is the happy ending to many biblical stories. When Jesus entered the scene, he told people to abide in him. In other words, there's no reason to wander. Your dwelling place is right here, in him. You and I might not be on a pilgrimage to find home, but we all can relate to searching for a happy ending to settle into. Jesus didn't point to a set of circumstances or

---

* Philippians 3:20.
† 1 Peter 2:11.

a plot on the map; he pointed to himself. It turns out, we can feel settled if our hearts settle into the right person, not the right place.

Looking back I don't see Florida as a detour or a slump (although I felt that way at the time). In retrospect I see the fingerprints of God's purpose: I found my kids there, I made lifelong friends there, I grew in my calling and career (and stopped wearing so many blouses), and most important, I grew in my soul.

The growth in my soul was evident the day I received a difficult call from a social worker. The call was about the biological father of the children we adopted. He passed away from a brain aneurysm. I knew the gravity of what this news would mean to them: another parent gone, another loss, another reminder that people leave and never come back. The news felt like the worst interruption to their healing journeys. Amid the smiles of soccer practice and the pirouettes on pointe shoes, the laughter at the dinner table and the honor roll certificate hanging on the fridge, healing would come to a screeching halt.

Up until that point I felt like God had picked the wrong person. But as I prepared to share the hard news with my kids, I thought for the first time, *I was made for this.* Not because of homemade organic smoothies or Mary Poppins perfection but because I understood the weight and pain of losing a parent far too early. I never felt like the perfect person for any job. But this situation, this grief, I knew this. I knew the weight, the complexity, the trauma, and the pain. This heart-holding job? I was the perfect person, even if I didn't want to be. I was qualified because of my weakness, not because of my strength. I understood the road ahead, the way the unannounced houseguest of grief would visit on graduations, wedding days, baby showers, and humdrum days too. I knew from experience (even though their relationship with their biological father was complicated) that there would be days when they would grieve what could have been.

Second Corinthians 3:5 says, "It is not that we think we are qualified to do anything on our own. Our qualification comes from God" (NLT). I spent so much time tallying up all the ways I felt unqualified, but this verse is a reminder that my qualification comes from God and what he's done in my life. I was able to hold their heavy hearts because mine had been held. I was able to help them through trauma because God took me on a journey to heal my own.

Though the news was painful, it didn't stop their progress. They keep progressing, growing, smiling, and laughing. Healing is a marathon, not a sprint, but I was there on that hard day, and I will be there on the hard days ahead. I'm not a perfect mom, but I'm a mom who understands.

Around the time we adopted, my hurt burst open as I heard about children in foster care having to sleep in social workers' offices because there weren't enough foster homes. I learned that half of the homeless population in our country have a history in foster care. And how 31 percent to 46 percent of youth who age out of foster care become homeless by age twenty-six.[3] With over 400,000 kids currently in foster care in the United States, over 117,000 of them are awaiting a forever family.[4]

I know not everyone is called to foster or adopt, but I fear that when we keep focusing on what we *can't* do, we are prevented from considering what we *can* do. And we can all do something to support vulnerable children. Like me, maybe you keep thinking about how unqualified you feel or how you don't measure up to Mary Poppins perfection. But the truth is, these kids were never asking for perfection; they just want someone to love them.

A few years after the adoption, I asked my daughter what her favorite family memories were so far. She said, "The time we all went bowling, and my brother was so mad, because he barely got any pins. And on Easter when you hid the eggs too good, and we could barely find any. And that time when we all played Watch Ya' Mouth, and I slobbered all over the table." Did you notice how all her favorite memories were the imperfect ones? I spent so much time trying to be the perfect mom when they arrived, but the best memories were the ones that included attitudes, mishaps, and slobber. It turns out, God didn't need my perfect plans, he needed only my willingness. I guess he knew what he was doing after all.

When you're in the messy middle, you see more fog and frustration than you do fingerprints. But if you're there right now—in a Bittersweet Season or a Season of Building or Balancing—this is my promise to you: You will not always feel this way. As someone who made it out of the vortex of change fatigue, I promise you that one day you will see the fingerprints too. One day you will look back on the divine connections made, the quiet breakthroughs, and the plot points of purpose woven into your story. You'll notice more glimmers of gratitude, remember how God strengthened you when you felt stuck, and recognize the rhythms that brought wholeness. And one day, as you're packing up to enter a new season, you'll realize you're not the same person who walked in. You're stronger, softer, wiser, and closer to God, and you're taking all that growth with you. You'll look back on a chapter you wouldn't want to go through again—but also wouldn't change—and think, *This is what I prayed for and so much more.*

ACKNOWLEDGMENTS

I once watched an interview in which an author was asked how he knew he was supposed to write another book. He said, "When I was haunted."

I resonate with those words. Over time it became clear that the Holy Spirit would not let me move on from this topic. I kept looking around to see if anyone else was talking about change fatigue or the unexpected weight of living in an answered prayer. (Maybe then I could show God someone more qualified to write the book, and I would stop being haunted.) But no one was. And the idea became like a shadow that followed me wherever I went. Since it wouldn't go away, I eventually conceded. So thank you, God. I give you permission to haunt me with many more book ideas, and I'll try not to drag my feet next time.

If this book were left solely up to me, it would be a whimsical mishmash with no pathway to transformation. Thankfully, along the way, God brought along an amazing team of people who helped me bring the book to life in the most beautiful and collaborative way.

To my literary agent, Blythe Daniel, thank you for not settling for anything less than the best of what this book could be. You helped me refine the message in a way that I never could have done on my own. You are a gift, and I am so grateful that you believed in me and this project.

To my editor, Brigitta Nortker, the day I got to meet you over Zoom is anchored as one of my favorite memories. Writing can feel like lonely work sometimes, but in that call I felt seen, understood, and empowered. You helped turn my abstract concepts into something concrete, and all the best parts of the book have your touch on them. Thank you for who you are and all you do.

To my production editor, Kathryn Duke, you are proof of God's unique fingerprint. Thank you for caring about every word and every line. I've heard countless stories from authors who worked with editors who removed their voice entirely, but you aimed to preserve mine and the heart of the message. You are a gem that I don't take for granted.

To the marketing team at Nelson Books—Kristen Golden, Lisa Beech, Lisbeth Keen—I am immensely grateful for your support, encouragement, and hard work. Thank you, Sydney Mathieu, for bringing the audiobook to life, and thank you, Lindy Kasler, for creating a cover I can't stop staring at. I appreciate each and every one of you.

Greg and Julie, if I didn't care about redundancy, this book would contain the line, "Here's what I learned from my mentors, Greg and Julie Gorman," in every chapter. You've imparted so much value to my life. Thank you for being my home away from home, and a soft place to land. Your Get Authorized course is what solidified my calling as a writer, and I'm immensely grateful.

Thank you to every person who allowed me to use their story in the book: Rachael Williams, Matt Lavier, Brianne Magee, Ryan Hallett, Jenee Robinson, Hannah Panza, and Kathy Peck (a.k.a. Gigi). Vulnerably sharing your real story is not easy in a culture that prefers the fairy-tale version. I'm grateful we got to partner together to move the needle toward hope-filled authenticity.

To my husband, thank you for being on the journey with me over the years as my clumsy little writing hobby became a calling, a passion, and a profession. Through every writing day and every writer's conference, you've been behind the scenes cheering me on and holding down a fort full of kiddos. Your support means the world. I love you.

To my children, thank you for letting me share my story as I know it's intertwined with yours (I know sometimes it can be embarrassing when your friends find me on Instagram). But I hope when you hold my book in your hands, it serves as a reminder of how much I treasure being your mom.

And last, I want to acknowledge a few faithful readers. Melissa Bryant, you have been reading (and championing) my writing since the early days when it wasn't anything worth reading. Pam Hatchell, you always seem to drop a word of encouragement on my posts on the days I only hear crickets. And to my family—my mom and sisters especially—thanks for always being in my corner, sharing my work, and believing in me.

And if you made it this far and read the entire book, I'm truly humbled. Thank you!

APPENDIX

Scriptures for the Four Seasons of Blessing

VERSES FOR SEASONS OF BLOOMING

But blessed is the one who trusts in the Lord,
whose confidence is in him.
They will be like a tree planted by the water
that sends out its roots by the stream.
It does not fear when heat comes;
its leaves are always green.
It has no worries in a year of drought
and never fails to bear fruit.

JEREMIAH 17:7–8

I am the vine; you are the branches. If you remain in me and I in you, you will bear much fruit.

JOHN 15:5

The Lord has done great things for us,
and we are filled with joy.

PSALM 126:3

He makes me lie down in green pastures,
he leads me beside still waters,
he refreshes my soul.

PSALM 23:2–3

God is able to bless you abundantly, so that in all things at all times, having all that you need, you will abound in every good work.

2 CORINTHIANS 9:8

Whatever you do, whether in word or deed, do it all in the name of the Lord Jesus, giving thanks to God the Father through him.

COLOSSIANS 3:17

VERSES FOR SEASONS OF BUILDING

Come to me, all you who are weary and burdened, and I will give you rest. Take my yoke upon you and learn from me, for I am gentle and humble in heart, and you will find rest for your souls. For my yoke is easy and my burden is light.

MATTHEW 11:28–30

Those who hope in the Lord
will renew their strength.
They will soar on wings like eagles;
they will run and not grow weary,
they will walk and not be faint.

ISAIAH 40:31

Always give yourselves fully to the work of the Lord, because you know that your labor in the Lord is not in vain.

1 CORINTHIANS 15:58

Let us not become weary in doing good, for at the proper time we will reap a harvest if we do not give up.

GALATIANS 6:9

Whatever you do, work at it with all your heart, as working for the Lord, not for human masters, since you know that you will receive an inheritance from the Lord as a reward. It is the Lord Christ you are serving.

COLOSSIANS 3:23–24

But he said to me, "My grace is sufficient for you, for my power is made perfect in weakness." Therefore I will boast all the more gladly about my weaknesses, so that Christ's power may rest on me.

2 CORINTHIANS 12:9

So do not fear, for I am with you;
  do not be dismayed, for I am your God.
I will strengthen you and help you;
  I will uphold you with my righteous right hand.

ISAIAH 41:10

Have I not commanded you? Be strong and courageous. Do not be frightened, and do not be dismayed, for the LORD your God is with you wherever you go.

JOSHUA 1:9 ESV

My flesh and my heart may fail,
  but God is the strength of my heart
  and my portion forever.

PSALM 73:26

I can do all this through him who gives me strength.

PHILIPPIANS 4:13

Additional reading: the book of Nehemiah

VERSES FOR BITTERSWEET SEASONS

Every good and perfect gift is from above, coming down from the Father of the heavenly lights, who does not change like shifting shadows.

JAMES 1:17

Be joyful in hope, patient in affliction, faithful in prayer.

ROMANS 12:12

Though the fig tree does not bud
  and there are no grapes on the vines . . .
yet I will rejoice in the LORD,
  I will be joyful in God my Savior.

HABAKKUK 3:17–18

The LORD is close to the brokenhearted
  and saves those who are crushed in spirit.

PSALM 34:18

We are hard pressed on every side, but not crushed; perplexed, but not in despair; persecuted, but not abandoned; struck down, but not destroyed.

2 CORINTHIANS 4:8–9

Why, my soul, are you downcast?
    Why so disturbed within me?
Put your hope in God,
    for I will yet praise him,
    my Savior and my God.

PSALM 42:11

Praise be to the God and Father of our Lord Jesus Christ, the Father of compassion and the God of all comfort, who comforts us in all our troubles, so that we can comfort those in any trouble with the comfort we ourselves receive from God.

2 CORINTHIANS 1:3–4

VERSES FOR SEASONS OF BALANCING

I the Lord do not change.

MALACHI 3:6

Jesus Christ is the same yesterday and today and forever.

HEBREWS 13:8

The grass withers and the flowers fall,
    but the word of our God endures forever.

ISAIAH 40:8

But the plans of the Lord stand firm forever,
the purposes of his heart through all generations.

PSALM 33:11

Remember the former things, those of long ago;
I am God, and there is no other;
I am God, and there is none like me.
I make known the end from the beginning,
from ancient times, what is still to come.

ISAIAH 46:9–10

If we are faithless,
he remains faithful,
for he cannot disown himself.

2 TIMOTHY 2:13

Do not be anxious about anything, but in every situation, by prayer and petition, with thanksgiving, present your requests to God. And the peace of God, which transcends all understanding, will guard your hearts and your minds in Christ Jesus.

PHILIPPIANS 4:6–7

I will be with you.

EXODUS 3:12

But God chose the foolish things of the world to shame the wise.

1 CORINTHIANS 1:27

Not that we are competent in ourselves, but our competence comes from God.

2 CORINTHIANS 3:5

Being confident of this, that he who began a good work in you will carry it on to completion.

PHILIPPIANS 1:6

Additional reading: Exodus 3–4, 14:10–12, 15:22–24, 17:3–4, Numbers 11:10–15, 14:1–4, 20:2–5

Declarations for the Four Seasons of Blessing

DECLARATIONS FOR SEASONS OF BLOOMING

I will not get complacent on the mountaintop. I will continue to seek God with all my heart.

I do not put my trust in outcomes or blessing; I put my trust in God.

I will trust God when I don't get what I pray for, and I will trust him when I get everything I pray for.

I rely on God's grace to help me carry every assignment and blessing he brings.

I won't hold back telling the stories of God's faithfulness and taking every opportunity to bring God glory.

I notice others who are struggling and share God's overflowing joy, peace, and light.

I will not bloom on the outside and wilt on the inside. I maintain healthy rhythms that sustain me in every season.

DECLARATIONS FOR SEASONS OF BUILDING

I rely on God's grace and supernatural enablement for what he has called me to do.

I will not toil or strive. I will remain Spirit-led in all that I do.

Both my work and my rest bring God glory.

There is room for everything God has called me to do. When I feel that I'm not enough, I know he is enough.

God's grace is sufficient for each day. I will not worry about tomorrow.

I take care of my mind, body, spirit, and soul, because God cares about my wholeness.

God will give me everything I need for my assignment.

DECLARATIONS FOR BITTERSWEET SEASONS

God invites my honest feelings. I can bring my gratitude and my grief to him, and he will always help me find my way forward.

Just because my heart feels broken doesn't mean I am broken. God gives me permission to be human and bring all my tears to him.

There is a time for everything. God will show me when it's time to grieve and when it's time to lean into gratitude.

Just because my heart aches doesn't mean I'm not grateful. I accept both truths and give myself grace.

Tending to my emotions in a healthy way is not a waste of time. It will impact generations.

This season will not last forever. I will lean into God and get stronger every day.

DECLARATIONS FOR SEASONS OF BALANCING

I can trust God with my confusing feelings. I never have to pretend with him.

My feelings are real, but they aren't final. I trust God and the story he is writing in my life.

My feelings can provide clues, not conclusions. I seek God for the truth.

The Holy Spirit gives me the discernment to know the difference between his leading and my feelings.

God is leading me on a journey toward wholeness, and I yield to him every step of the way.

I am not stuck; I am strong.

Practical Tools for the Four Seasons of Blessing

BOOKS FOR SEASONS OF BLOOMING

Practicing the Way: Be with Jesus. Become Like Him. Do as He Did. by John Mark Comer

Growing Slow: Lessons on Un-Hurrying Your Heart from an Accidental Farm Girl by Jennifer Dukes Lee

BOOKS FOR SEASONS OF BUILDING

Soul Keeping: Caring for the Most Important Part of You by John Ortberg

Emotionally Healthy Spirituality: It's Impossible to Be Spiritually Mature While Remaining Emotionally Immature by Peter Scazzero

BOOKS FOR BITTERSWEET SEASONS

The Garden Within: Where the War with Your Emotions Ends and Your Most Powerful Life Begins by Dr. Anita Phillips

Soul Care: Find Life-Giving Rhythms, Live Restored, Avoid Burnout, Discover Unspeakable Joy by Debra Fileta

BOOKS FOR SEASONS OF BALANCING

I Shouldn't Feel This Way: Name What's Hard, Tame Your Guilt, and Transform Self-Sabotage into Brave Action by Dr. Alison Cook

Try Softer: A Fresh Approach to Move Us out of Anxiety, Stress, and Survival Mode—and into a Life of Connection and Joy by Aundi Kolber

HELPFUL RESOURCES IN ALL FOUR SEASONS

A guided journal: *Sacred Prayer: 90 Days of Deeper Intimacy with God* by Ann Voskamp

A daily devotional: *Emotionally Healthy Spirituality Day by Day: A 40-Day Journey with the Daily Office* by Peter Scazzero

A breath-prayer guide and devotional: *Breath as Prayer: Calm Your Anxiety, Focus Your Mind, and Renew Your Soul* by Jennifer Tucker

Biblical inner healing modality: HeartSync, HeartSyncHealing.org/

Christian therapy: Debra Fileta Counselors Network, DebraFileta.com/Counseling

FIVE W.H.O.L.E. QUESTIONS TO ASK GOD DAILY

W: Wellness—God, how do you want me to care for my body today?

H: Heart—God, how do you want me to tend to my heart today?

O: Outlook—God, what lie needs to be replaced with truth today?

L: Life with God—God, how do you want to connect with me today?

E: Engagement—God, who do you want me to call or encourage today?

NOTES

CHAPTER 1: YOUR PRAYER WAS ANSWERED—NOW WHAT?

1. Thomas H. Holmes and Richard H. Rahe, "The Social Readjustment Rating Scale," *Journal of Psychosomatic Research* 11, no. 2 (1967): 213–18, https://doi.org/10.1016/0022-3999(67)90010-4.
2. Shauna Niequist, *Bittersweet: Thoughts on Change, Grace, and Learning the Hard Way* (Zondervan, 2020), 83.
3. Jeremy B. Bernerth et al., "Change Fatigue: Development and Initial Validation of a New Measure," *Work & Stress: An International Journal of Work, Health & Organisations* 25, no. 4 (2011): 321–37, https://doi.org/10.1080/02678373.2011.634280.
4. Simon Kemp, "Digital 2024: Global Overview Report," DataReportal, January 31, 2024, https://datareportal.com/reports/digital-2024-global-overview-report; Bureau of Labor Statistics, "American Time Use Survey—2023 Results," US Department of Labor, June 21, 2024, PDF, 9, https://www.bls.gov/news.release/archives/atus_06272024.pdf.
5. Johann Hari, *Stolen Focus: Why You Can't Pay Attention—and How to Think Deeply Again*, narrated by Johann Hari (Random House Audio, 2022), at 9 hr., 32 min.

CHAPTER 2: WHAT DID YOU EXPECT?

1. Wolfram Shultz et al., "A Neural Substrate of Prediction and Reward," *Science* 275, no. 5306 (1997): 1593–99, https://doi.org/10.1126/science.275.5306.1593.

2. John C. Maxwell, *Put Your Dream to the Test: 10 Questions to Help You See It and Seize It* (Thomas Nelson, 2009), xv.
3. Stephanie DeFord et al., "A Review of Literature on Substance Abuse Among Anaesthesia Providers," *Journal of Research in Nursing* 24, no. 8 (2019): 587–600, https://doi.org/10.1177/1744987119827353.

CHAPTER 3: GOOD GRIEF!

1. Sylvia L. Mikucki-Enyart, "Why Post-Wedding Depression Is So Common," *Psychology Today*, July 15, 2022, https://www.psychologytoday.com/us/blog/communicating-through-change/202207/why-post-wedding-depression-is-so-common.
2. Rosemary Black, "What Is Post-Wedding Depression?," HealthCentral, July 31, 2023, https://www.healthcentral.com/condition/depression/post-wedding-depression.
3. Sarah Sloat, "Post-Wedding Anxiety Is 'Really Common.' Here's How to Cope," *The Guardian*, July 11, 2024, https://www.theguardian.com/wellness/article/2024/jul/11/post-wedding-anxiety-coping.
4. Anne-Laure Le Cunff, "The Comedown Effect: Understanding the Emotional Aftermath of Achievement," Ness Labs, accessed January 8, 2026, https://nesslabs.com/comedown-effect.
5. *Extreme Engagement*, season 1, episode 6, "The Crying Game," directed by PJ Madam, featuring Tim Noonan and PJ Madam, aired on July 12, 2019, on Netflix, https://www.netflix.com/title/80210245.
6. "Post-Race Blues: The Neuroscience of Marathon Recovery," Abbott, April 4, 2023, https://www.abbott.com/corpnewsroom/nutrition-health-and-wellness/post-race-blues-the-neuroscience-of-marathon-recovery.html.
7. "Postpartum Depression," Cleveland Clinic, last reviewed on April 12, 2022, https://my.clevelandclinic.org/health/diseases/9312-postpartum-depression.
8. Henry Cloud, "Learn the Three 'P's' of Negative Thinking | Dr. Henry Cloud," posted on June 21, 2023, by The

Dr. Cloud Show, YouTube, https://www.youtube.com/watch?v=tEeHCaJ9roU.

9. *The Gorge*, directed by Scott Derrickson, featuring Miles Teller and Anya Taylor-Joy, 2025, Apple TV, https://tv.apple.com/us/movie/the-gorge/umc.cmc.26o403koqo2klixc0jtqy6tmc.
10. Brené Brown, "The Power of Vulnerability," TEDxHouston, June 2010, 15:39, https://www.ted.com/talks/brene_brown_the_power_of_vulnerability.

CHAPTER 4: GRATITUDE, GLIMMERS, GEMS, AND GUARDRAILS

1. John Mark Comer, *The Ruthless Elimination of Hurry: How to Stay Emotionally Healthy and Spiritually Alive in the Chaos of the Modern World* (Waterbrook, 2019), 52.
2. Jennifer Dukes Lee, *Growing Slow: Lessons on Un-Hurrying Your Heart from an Accidental Farm Girl* (Zondervan, 2021), 4.
3. A. J. Swoboda, *The Dusty Ones: Why Wandering Deepens Your Faith* (Baker Books, 2016), 77.
4. Maureen Salamon, "Gratitude Enhances Health, Brings Happiness—and May Even Lengthen Lives," Harvard Health, September 11, 2024, https://www.health.harvard.edu/blog/gratitude-enhances-health-brings-happiness-and-may-even-lengthen-lives-202409113071.
5. John Ortberg, *The Life You're Always Wanted: Spiritual Disciplines for Ordinary People*, rev. ed. (Zondervan, 2002), 77.
6. Russell Conwell, "Acres of Diamonds," Temple University, accessed January 9, 2026, https://www.temple.edu/about/history/acres-diamonds.

CHAPTER 5: YOU'RE NOT STUCK; YOU'RE STRONG

1. Lisa Robinson, "Adele, Queen of Hearts," *Vanity Fair*, October 31, 2016, https://www.vanityfair.com/culture/2016/10/adele-cover-story?mbid=synd_glamour.

2. Daniel Schorn, "Tom Brady: The Winner," CBS News, November 3, 2005, https://www.cbsnews.com/news/tom-brady-the-winner/.
3. Susan Scutti, "Michael Phelps: 'I Am Extremely Thankful That I Did Not Take My Life,'" CNN, updated January 20, 2019, https://www.cnn.com/2018/01/19/health/michael-phelps-depression.
4. Jann S. Wenner, *Lennon Remembers: The Full Rolling Stone Interviews from 1970* (Straight Arrow, 1971; repr., Verso, 2000).
5. Jon Krakauer, *Into Thin Air: A Personal Account of the Mount Everest Disaster* (Villard, 1997).
6. *Golf Digest* (@GolfDigest), "Scottie went down a rabbit hole on this one," Facebook, July 15, 2025, https://www.facebook.com/watch/?v=1080310206799707.
7. Richard Brown, "Post-Achievement Depression: Overcoming the Slump," *Psychology Today*, May 17, 2024, https://www.psychologytoday.com/us/blog/understanding-health-behaviors/202405/post-achievement-depression-overcoming-the-slump.
8. C. S. Lewis, *Mere Christianity* (Geoffrey Bles, 1952; repr., HarperCollins, 2023), 136–37.
9. Nick Cady, "Augustine and Disordered Loves," *Theology for the People* (blog), April 11, 2019, https://nickcady.org/2019/04/11/augustine-disordered-loves/.

CHAPTER 6: THE BEST KIND OF CHANGE

1. C. S. Lewis, *Letters of C. S. Lewis*, ed. W. H. Lewis and Walter Hooper, rev. ed. (Harcourt, 1966; repr., HarperOne, 1993), 610.
2. Herminia Ibarra and Otilia Obodaru, "Betwixt and Between Identities: Liminal Experience in Contemporary Careers," INSEAD Working Paper Series, no. 2016/79/OBH (November 2016), https://doi.org/10.2139/ssrn.2866988.
3. Viktor E. Frankl, *Man's Search for Meaning: An Introduction to Logotherapy*, trans. Ilse Lasch (Beacon Press, 2006), 66.
4. Jim Forest, *The Ladder of the Beatitudes* (Orbis, 1999), 35.
5. Mark Nelson et al., "Using a Closed Ecological System to Study

Earth's Biosphere: Initial Results from Biosphere 2," *BioScience* 43, no. 4 (1993): 225–36, https://doi.org/10.2307/1312123.

6. Bruce Feiler, *Life Is in the Transitions: Mastering Change at Any Age* (Penguin, 2020), 312.
7. W. Richard Walker et al., "On the Emotions That Accompany Autobiographical Memories: Dysphoria Disrupts the Fading Affect Bias," *Cognition and Emotion* 17, no. 5 (2010): 703–23, https://doi.org/10.1080/02699930302287.

CHAPTER 7: NEW BEGINNINGS

1. Pam Rosewell Moore, *Life Lessons from the Hiding Place: Discovering the Heart of Corrie ten Boom* (Chosen, 2004), 53.
2. Daniel A. Miller, *The Gifts of Acceptance: Embracing People and Things as They Are* (Ebb and Flow, 2018), 167.
3. Emily Glover, "How Long Does It Take to Get Used to Being a Mom? 4 Months and 23 Days, Says Survey," *Motherly*, April 25, 2022, https://www.mother.ly/parenting/how-long-does-it-take-to-get-used-to-being-a-mom-4-months-and-23-days-says-survey/.
4. John C. Maxwell, *The 15 Invaluable Laws of Growth: Live Them and Reach Your Potential*, 10th anniv. ed. (Center Street, 2022), 165.
5. Henri J. M. Nouwen, *Here and Now: Living in the Spirit* (Crossroad, 2003), 16.
6. Lisa Harper, "In a World Where Horrible Things Happen, Where Does Happiness Fit?," *Ann Voskamp* (blog), June 2017, https://annvoskamp.com/2017/06/in-a-world-where-horrible-things-happen-where-does-happiness-fit/.

CHAPTER 8: IF PRAYER GOT YOU HERE . . .

1. Francine Shapiro, "Eye Movement Desensitization: A New Treatment For PostTraumatic Stress Disorder," *Journal of Behavior Therapy and Experimental Psychiatry* 20, no. 3 (1989): 211–17, https://doi.org/10.1016/0005-7916(89)90025-6.
2. Laura Schober, "What Happens to Your Blood Pressure When You Walk Every Day?," *Health*, June 26, 2025, https://www.health

.com/blood-pressure-and-walking-11750887; Hannah Roberts et al., "The Effect of Short-Term Exposure to the Natural Environment on Depressive Mood: A Systematic Review and Meta-Analysis," *Environmental Research* 177 (October 2019), https://doi.org/10.1016/j.envres.2019.108606; Gregory N. Bratman et al., "Nature Experience Reduces Rumination and Subgenual Prefrontal Cortex Activation," *The Proceedings of the National Academy of Sciences* 112, no. 28 (2015): 8567–72, https://doi.org/10.1073/pnas.1510459112.

3. Vijay R. Varma et al., "Low-Intensity Daily Walking Activity Is Associated with Hippocampal Volume in Older Adults," *Hippocampus* 25, no. 5 (2014): 605–15, https://doi.org/10.1002/hipo.22397.
4. Marily Oppezzo and Daniel L. Schwartz, "Give Your Ideas Some Legs: The Positive Effect of Walking on Creative Thinking," *Journal of Experimental Psychology: Learning, Memory, and Cognition* 40, no. 4 (2014): 1142–52, https://psycnet.apa.org/doi/10.1037/a0036577.
5. Hyunju Jo et al., "Physiological and Psychological Effects of Forest and Urban Sounds Using High-Resolution Sound Sources," *International Journal of Environmental Research and Public Health* 16, no. 15 (2019): 2649, https://doi.org/10.3390/ijerph16152649.
6. Ryan Hamilton, "Ryan Hamilton Stand-Up," posted on September 11, 2019, by The Tonight Show Starring Jimmy Fallon, YouTube, 0:43, https://www.youtube.com/watch?v=QncQNabfRL0.
7. C. S. Lewis, *Letters of C. S. Lewis*, ed. W. H. Lewis and Walter Hooper, rev. ed. (Harcourt, 1966; repr., HarperOne, 1993), 365–66.
8. Kosuke Koyama, *Three Mile an Hour God: Biblical Reflections* (Orbis, 1980), 1.
9. Elizabeth Bernstein, "The Science of Prayer," *The Wall Street Journal*, May 17, 2020, https://www.wsj.com/articles/the-science-of-prayer-11589720400.
10. Amy B. Wachholtz and Kenneth I. Pargament, "Is Spirituality a Critical Ingredient of Meditation? Comparing the Effects of

Spiritual Meditation, Secular Meditation, and Relaxation on Spiritual, Psychological, Cardiac, and Pain Outcomes," *Journal of Behavioral Medicine* 28, no. 4 (2005): 369–84, https://doi.org/10.1007/s10865-005-9008-5.

11. Luciano Bernardi et al., "Effect of Rosary Prayer and Yoga Mantras on Autonomic Cardiovascular Rhythms: Comparative Study," *British Medical Journal* 323, no. 7327 (2001): 1446–49, https://doi.org/10.1136/bmj.323.7327.1446.
12. L. H. Powell et al., "Religion and Spirituality: Linkages to Physical Health," *American Psychologist* 58, no. 1 (2003): 36–52, https://psycnet.apa.org/doi/10.1037/0003-066X.58.1.36.
13. Kevin S. Masters and Glen I. Spielmans, "Prayer and Health: Review, Meta-Analysis, and Research Agenda," *Journal of Behavioral Medicine* 30 (May 2007): 329–38, https://doi.org/10.1007/s10865-007-9106-7.
14. Daniel J. Siegel and Tina Payne Bryson, *The Whole-Brain Child: 12 Revolutionary Strategies to Nurture Your Child's Developing Mind, Survive Everyday Parenting Struggles, and Help Your Family Thrive* (Delacorte, 2011), 41.

CHAPTER 9: LIVING W.H.O.L.E.: RHYTHMS THAT RESTORE

1. Wayne Muller, *Sabbath: Finding Rest, Renewal, and Delight in Our Busy Lives* (Bantam, 1999), 68.
2. Dan W. Grupe and Jack B. Nitschke, "Uncertainty and Anticipation in Anxiety: An Integrated Neurobiological and Psychological Perspective," *Nature Reviews Neuroscience* 14 (June 2013): 488–501, https://doi.org/10.1038/nrn3524.
3. Julie Mullins, host, *So Good Sisterhood*, podcast, season 5, episode 7, "Turning the Page on Depression and Anxiety with Deb Fileta—Part 1," Christ Fellowship Church, March 19, 2023, https://www.christfellowship.church/so-good-sisterhood/season-5-episode-7.
4. Anita Phillips, *The Garden Within: Where the War with Your Emotions Ends and Your Most Powerful Life Begins* (Zondervan, 2024), xviii.

5. Phillips, *Garden Within*, xxv.
6. Matthew Fox, *Illuminations of Hildegard of Bingen* (Bear & Company, 1985), 99.
7. Fox, *Hildegard of Bingen*, 30.
8. Peter Scazzero, *Emotionally Healthy Spirituality: It's Impossible to Be Spiritually Mature While Remaining Emotionally Immature*, updated ed. (Zondervan, 2017), 19.
9. John Mark Comer, *The Ruthless Elimination of Hurry: How to Stay Emotionally Healthy and Spiritually Alive in the Chaos of the Modern World* (Waterbrook, 2019), 155.
10. Dan Buettner, *The Blue Zones: Lessons for Living Longer from the People Who've Lived the Longest* (National Geographic, 2008), 89–91.
11. Simone Schnall et al., "Social Support and the Perception of Geographical Slant," *Journal of Experimental Social Psychology* 44, no. 5 (2008): 1246–55, https://doi.org/10.1016/j.jesp.2008.04.011.

CONCLUSION

1. Susan Krauss Whitbourne, "10 Ways to Make It Through Your Life's Transitions," *Psychology Today*, March 14, 2017, https://www.psychologytoday.com/us/blog/fulfillment-at-any-age/201703/10-ways-to-make-it-through-your-lifes-transitions.
2. Karalyn F. Enz et al., "The Relocation Bump: Memories of Middle Adulthood Are Organized Around Residential Moves," *Journal of Experimental Psychology: General* 145, no. 8 (2016): 935–40, https://psycnet.apa.org/doi/10.1037/xge0000188.
3. Amy Dworsky et al., "Homelessness During the Transition from Foster Care to Adulthood," *American Journal of Public Health* 103 (November 2013), https://doi.org/10.2105/AJPH.2013.301455.
4. "About the Children," AdoptUSKids, accessed September 22, 2025, https://adoptuskids.org/meet-the-children/about-the-children.

ABOUT THE AUTHOR

Melissa Miller is a family girl, writer, and Reboot Retreat facilitator living in Tennessee. She is a contributor to sites such as *Mother.ly*, *Her View from Home*, and the YouVersion Bible app. Melissa has been married for over twenty years, has five children, and is an advocate for vulnerable children in foster care. Having experienced an unconventional adoption as a teen and later adopting a sibling set from foster care, she has a heart to help kids from hard places find belonging. Melissa loves playing pickleball and thinks "just one more chapter" is a perfectly reasonable bedtime strategy. Through her writing and two-day Reboot Retreat process, she loves helping people step out of survival mode, establish life-giving rhythms, and rediscover joy in their everyday lives.

CONNECT WITH MELISSA

Website: MelissaMillerWriter.com

Weekly Newsletter: MelissaMiller.Substack.com

Instagram: @MelissaMillerWrites